A Hand to Hold

ALSO BY COLEEN NOLAN

Upfront and Personal: The Autobiography
Live. Laugh. Love: Lessons I've Learned
No Regrets
Mum to Mum: Happy Memories and Honest Advice
Denial
Envy

COLEEN NOLAN

WITH JULIE SHAW

A Hand to Hold

ALL I'VE LEARNT ABOUT GRIEF

Harper
North

HarperNorth
Windmill Green
24 Mount Street
Manchester M2 3NX

A division of
HarperCollins*Publishers*
1 London Bridge Street
London SE1 9GF

www.harpercollins.co.uk

HarperCollinsPublishers
Macken House
39/40 Mayor Street Upper
Dublin 1
D01 C9W8

First published by HarperNorth in 2024

1 3 5 7 9 10 8 6 4 2

A catalogue record for this book
is available from the British Library

HB ISBN: 978-0-00-870597-8
TPB ISBN: 978-0-00-871620-2

Printed and bound in the UK using 100%
renewable electricity at CPI Group (UK) Ltd, Croydon

To all of you that read and need this book

CONTENTS

FOREWORD

PLEASE BELIEVE ME when I say I know about grief. In fact you could say grief and I have a personal, long-term relationship. Many of us find it hard to talk about loss, but it's something that all of us face at some point. Bereavement survivors – it's a club we will all join, even when we hope we won't. What we don't know is when. My first really notable experience with grief was when my sister in law, Linzie, died suddenly in 1991, after contracting a viral infection. She was only 26 years old – the same age as I was – and it was such a terrible shock, it shook me to the core. All these years later in fact, I don't think I'll ever get over that first sudden grief; it will haunt me forever.

But perhaps it meant that I couldn't avoid the subject – while my family and everyone who knew Linzie were trying to come to terms with their loss, I saw how hard people found it to know what to say to us. I think, from then on, I knew I wanted to be able to say a few words to other people who found themselves in my shoes. Of course, in the years between then and now, life has taken more people from me, and I've seen friends and loved ones go through many hard times. What stands out to me is that each grief is as unique as the life we mourn. And because of that, there's no one-size-fits-all approach when it comes to facing and living not just *with* but *through* grief. With sorrow or love, acceptance or denial, humour or rage, your own path through grief – whether you're religious or not, mourning a sudden loss or a long-awaited passing – is unique to you. The same is true whatever kind of loss you're facing – public or private, partner or friend, child or parent, the death of a pet or the passing of someone you had a complicated relationship with. There are no rules here. Instead, I wanted to share companionship and experience, options and validations. You may feel alone, but I hope this book helps you know that other people have walked this path, even if you can't see them right now.

In the intensity of grief, it can be hard to see that the loss can shape us almost as much as knowing the person did. I'm thinking in particular of 1998, when we lost our father, Tommy, to liver cancer, and then just a few years later, our lovely mum, Maureen, passed after suffering terribly from Alzheimer's disease. Mum's passing, or the lead up to it, was just awful. We had to watch as the woman we all knew and loved simply disappeared, and was replaced by an aggressive stranger who eventually didn't recognise any of us. I remember one night I lay with her in the home we'd had to put her in, and I thought, if there is a god, please let her pass peacefully – and quickly too, as I couldn't bear to see her suffer as she was. When she finally died, I acknowledged that perhaps He had heard me, because she did pass peacefully and, although it was heartbreaking, I also felt a huge sense of relief that she was no longer suffering.

Then, of course, our beautiful sister Bernie died in 2013, aged just 52, after a long and arduous battle with cancer. She also passed peacefully, surrounded by all of us, all the people she loved. That was devastating, but you know, Bernie will never be forgotten, we simply won't let that happen. We talk about her all the time, wherever we are, and we'll say things like, 'oh, Bernie would love this!' Or 'remember when Bernie did such and such.' It's both comforting and a bit sad, really, when we do this, but we won't stop it. We want to feel she's with us, always.

It was these experiences that really got me thinking about grief and how different people cope in different ways, and they are what spurred me on to create my podcasts on the subject. They have been an incredible chance to hear other people's stories. I got together with some of my friends, and chatted with them for hours on their own personal suffering and what they went through. It showed me how universal grief is – being in the public eye doesn't protect you from loss. These conversations were full of surprises – laughter as well as tears – and a hundred different ways to mourn. They also taught me that coping with grief isn't just a straight path. The emotions we go through can zigzag all over the place before we can eventually look back and realise that we've come out the other end. It was this realisation that inspired me to write this book, and I do hope that, as a reader, you can appreciate that I'm not trying to preach a gospel here; there is no right or wrong way to deal with such a horrible experience. Because of that, the chapters are written so you can read them straight through, but also you can dip in as you need them. While there are recognised stages of grief, grief itself isn't a straight line – you can't tick off the boxes – and so the order of these chapters reflects this. Everyone deals with it differently, and any stage can creep up on you at any time, or mixed up together. So this isn't a guidebook, more a companion – your way is okay.

Of course, music has been a huge part of my life, and I can't tell you the number of times a song has helped me express how I feel, lifted me in hard times or brought back happy memories. Because I know that sometimes lyrics or a poem can reach places other words can't, I've worked with fellow writer Julie Shaw to include a brief verse at the end of each chapter. Sometimes in grief it's hard to concentrate on anything for very long, and don't be surprised if you find yourself having to reread sections to fully take them in. If your thoughts are racing, then sometimes a poem can be a great place to start.

On my path through life, I've been lots of things: singer, performer, agony aunt, broadcaster, writer and interviewer. And while I'm not a professional grief counsellor, having been on my own journey and working closely with lots of experts (you'll find lots of resources at the back of the book), I wanted to share my stories and those of others to help you find words when they feel hard to come by, and for this book to feel like a hand reaching out to take yours.

Grief

How do you describe a word as big as grief?
We can't in simple language, but this is my belief:
It's a feeling of sheer helplessness, of the very deepest sorrow,
It's the knowledge that you've gone away, and we won't
see you tomorrow.
It's a searing pain, a catch of breath each time we say your name,
It's trying to get through just one day, knowing
the next will be the same.
It's the thoughts that flood our mind, uninvited, relentless, raw,
It's the unexpected triggers and crying until we're sore.
It's memories and glimpses of something we feel but do not know,
That if love's the highest mountain, this is the deep valley below.
Grief is such a simple word, yet in it we could sink,
But it ties us to our loved ones, the last and fiercest link.
And when we learn to walk with it and face that primal fear,
Then we know no-one's truly lost, if a thought can bring them near

Chapter 1

ONE STEP AT A TIME?

IT IS A well-known theory that there are five stages of grief, and most of us are familiar with them. Denial, anger, bargaining, depression and acceptance are all stages in this model of grief, and I would bet that at some point, we have all experienced these feelings. But models are exactly that – examples, guides, frameworks. You are more than a model; we all are glorious, complex, contradictory individuals, so don't worry if you don't fit or recognise each or any of these stages. You'll have your own steps to climb – up and down, or even many times over. It doesn't matter if these aren't precisely your stages, but it may help to put a name to some of the emotions likely to be storming through you. And they're not set in stone either. More recently it has been suggested that in fact there may be seven stages of grief, adding in 'reconstruction and working through' and 'the upward turn' before you reach acceptance and hope.

I like that these modern ways of looking at grief add in something new and that they seem quite positive in comparison to those earlier stages – which, let's be honest, can be quite horrific. Acceptance is a powerful and important feeling, but it doesn't help us turn our eyes to the future: something which hope does. Hope suggests that even in the darkest times, there will come movement and change, something to look forward to. A time we know will come when we can start moving forward – not forgetting, not ignoring, but looking ahead.

Although we talk about the stages of grief, and we see them written in an order, this is not how we always experience them. They can come and go in any order at all – often we will experience every single stage in one day, and then the next day we can go through any or all of them again in a different order. As I go through the book sharing my own stories and some from other familiar names and faces, you'll see we've all grieved in different ways, in different orders and in our own time – and you can too.

The initial grief is often an all-consuming hell. Either total numbness and disbelief; a physical pain and shock or the storms of crying; the animalistic instinct to curl up and wail, or hit out at someone. It can feel like no other pain we have ever endured, and we can't imagine that anyone else could comprehend how we feel. There can be an amplifying loop where everything we think about – every moment, memory or word – makes the pain feel larger and more raw. And when that peaks, that's frequently when the denial hits us – we simply can't believe that the person we loved is never coming back, that we will never see them again. This is very normal, and the detachment we feel is our body's way of protecting us until we can start to deal with the pain bit by bit. Some people go as far as to completely block the fact that they have suffered a loss and may carry on as if nothing has happened. There are no ticking clocks at this stage, no fixed points where you should be 'through' a feeling. More often than not, the emotions will come in waves. You might think you're back in calmer waters only for it to feel like the next wave knocks you off your feet.

For me, next came anger. When I lost my beloved sister-in-law at such a young age, I found myself screaming at an unjust god. Why would He take such a young, beautiful soul when there are evil people out there walking around as fit as fiddles? I think I told myself back then that there couldn't actually be a god, and that I no longer believed in him. Yet much, much later, when my mother was dying, bed-bound and ravaged by her Alzheimer's, I found myself turning to that same god and pleading with him to allow our mother a fast and peaceful death.

People can also feel anger towards the one who has died. I remember a friend of mine who lost her partner when they were in the middle of a big building project. She told me she stood in the mud, in the foundations of the house that was meant to be their forever home and shouted to the skies at him, so mad at him that he'd left her to build this alone. In the end, she built a beautiful home but I know how hard it was.

5

You might also feel angry at yourself. A friend of mine said that when her father had died she gave herself such a hard time for months afterwards, because of all the things she felt she should have said, or should have done. Allow yourself to feel the anger – we're often taught that it's a bad emotion, but it's natural to feel helpless if you're lacking closure, or wish circumstances had been different. Let the emotion be, and it's more likely to pass without weighing you down.

Bargaining is also often referred to as 'magical thinking', and this is because our minds can go completely haywire after such a loss and we can actually believe that if we do such and such or promise never to do whatever, then we can bring the person back to us. We make senseless deals with ourselves or our god, and at the time we really mean it. I've known others who have believed that, if they did certain things in certain ways, or did some good for others, then they would prevent anything bad happening to another loved one. Although in retrospect this kind of thinking may sound silly, it's actually part of the healing process and allows us to at least feel something other than hurt. Of course, we later realise that a miracle was never going to happen, but we believed it at the time. I will always remember when a friend almost died when she was giving birth. Her mum was in absolute bits, crying and pleading to God. She solemnly promised that if He saved her, she'd never miss a day of church ever again. Happily, she survived, and her mother went to church every day for the rest of her life!

The depression stage of grief is so hard to define as it involves so many different sensations and emotions. Your body can feel absolutely shattered, exhausted and as if it has suddenly aged by years. You may feel like you don't want to get out of bed and would rather sleep away your days so that you don't have to face reality. Guilt, loneliness, shock and deep sadness can all give way to depression. These are all very normal feelings, but if you find yourself in a pit that you are unable to climb out from, then please seek help. There are so many organisations out there – lots of which I will name and give details about in the final part of this book. After a dear friend of mine lost his wife he sank so low at one stage that he actually contemplated taking his own life. Depression had taken such a hold that he simply could not envisage a life without his love, and he even planned how he would do it, believing that we'd all understand. We absolutely would not have understood, we were all grieving too, in our own ways. I just can't imagine what that would have done to us. Thankfully, he decided to call the Samaritans at the last minute, and that was the start of his recovery. He recognised he needed help, and grabbed at it just in time. He went on to have regular counselling and says that this has helped immeasurably.

Acceptance is when it finally hits us that we will never physically see our lost loved one again, and that we have to find a different way of living from now on. It's not in a 'oh well, they're gone now, so I move on' type of way; it's more of a realisation that life for us, moving forward, is going to be completely different, but that actually it is possible for us to continue to live. This can be a very scary time, because we know now that anything we ever do from here on will be done without them. If we watch a new, exciting TV series, we won't have them to talk to about it. If we get a new job, they're not there to celebrate with. This all hits us in the acceptance stage, and yet still, bravely, we take the step. Some people find it comforting at this stage to revisit old memories. To take out photo albums and start to feel that connection with them again. Don't feel as though you're going a bit bonkers if you find yourself talking out loud to them at this stage, or any other – it's normal; it's how we deal with such an enormous loss, and it can be very therapeutic. Go for long walks, or to a church if that's your thing, just anywhere that you can have some peace alone to think about your loved one, and make sure to keep talking about them to others who knew them. Keeping the connection alive like this really does help, even if you can't be with them physically.

One of the less talked about stages of grief is the sixth on the model: reconstruction and working through. This is actually us processing it all, giving ourselves some goals or small steps that see us moving forward. It's a time when we feel that the worst is over; even though we are still sad, we recognise that we have finally accepted that our loss is something we must learn to live with. It might surprise you to learn that at this stage we should re-evaluate almost everything. We've neglected our bodies throughout this process and now we need to sort that out. Eating healthily, keeping hydrated and getting enough sleep are so important, and now is the time to get back on track. Some daily exercise, no matter how little, is also important, as is deep breathing and giving ourselves some time out that's just for us. Small goals are important, such as rehearsing how you will react to others now when they ask about your grief, so that you're prepared, and also being prepared to be the one to bring it up if necessary. Others might not be sure if you are ready to talk, but let them know it's important to you if that's what you want. Connect with others too, maybe join a support group or community group. Some people find that having a creative outlet allows them to express their grief, such as painting, drawing or writing. Anything you always promised yourself you'd eventually do, now is the time.

The final stage on the newer model is acceptance and hope. This is all about realising that you can't change the situation, but you can change your response to it. You can finally feel some control in how you react in social situations, within your family, or at work. You might find at this stage that, if you start to become overwhelmed again, you can actually place those feelings to one side while you get along with your day and are able to revisit them rationally at a later point. This is a huge achievement, and as time goes on, it becomes easier to do. Don't get me wrong, there will be days when you slip back into any one – or all – of those previous stages of grief, and it will feel that it is never-ending, but trust me, it won't last long compared to those early days, and you will be able to bring yourself out of it.

The stories you'll find in this book won't be the same as your story – but I hope they'll help you feel that your own encounters with grief are ones you can not only get through, but share when you're ready. We all know the old saying that a problem shared is a problem halved, and while grief is not a 'problem' and certainly not something that can be solved – it can definitely be transformed by sharing the emotions with someone. But if you're not ready for talking about it, then I hope that just knowing that people care and have been through similar circumstances will be a little pinprick of light – a first star in a dark sky, and a sign that you'll get through the night of grief and into the sunshine again one day. There are some tough stories in the pages ahead – I've never been one to pretend that life is all roses and I think it helps to acknowledge that. And alongside the tough stories, I hope you'll find plenty to smile about too, because, just like life, grief isn't made up of simple opposites or neatly boxed emotions – so whether you want to laugh, cry or shout out loud, I hope we can share our stories together.

Stage by stage

This can't be happening, it's just not true,
How can you be gone?
You were vibrant, full of life,
Surely this is wrong.

How could you ever leave me?
How dare you not be here?
You've left me all alone like this,
Filled with rage and fear.

If I had done things differently,
If I promise I'll do more,
Would this change the outcome?
Will you walk back through the door?

I just can't cope without you,
I don't know how to live,
To have you back beside me,
My very soul I'd give.

I know the facts, I've faced the truth,
But my heart needs time to heal,
A time of rest and gentle steps
As I accept it's real.

I know they say that love abides
Beyond the life we see,
And I'll be forever thankful
For all you gave to me.

Chapter 2

ADVANCE PLANNING

WHY IS IT that so many of us are reluctant to talk about the inevitable? The truth is that from the moment we are born, we are heading towards death, no matter how near or far away that might be. And just as you might plan for a big anniversary, for example, or where you'd like to be in ten years' time, it can be strangely liberating to think about what you might want for your funeral, or your possessions, after you're gone. Many of us are lucky enough to have family or friends who care, so by leaving some notes, thoughts, ideas or even formal plans, you leave a gift of thoughtfulness for those who will be left behind. It isn't morbid, really, although none of us like to imagine a time when we aren't here, but it actually makes sound sense.

Even so, it's often not until we really feel the grains of sand trickling through the hourglass that we actually start to plan. When some people know they are dying, and are still able to plan coherently, they will often try to remove some of the burden from their loved ones by planning their own funeral service. Our sister Bernie intricately planned her own celebration of life in minute detail. This took a huge amount of pressure away from the rest of us, and it was lovely that we even had moments during that service when we were laughing and hugging each other as we shared happier memories. The service itself was held in a theatre, can you imagine? Perfect for Bernie actually, and nothing could have been so fitting. For all of us, really. I mean, we have spent almost all of our lives in theatres around the country.

We knew for a long time that the sad day would come when we would lose Bernie, and although she spoke to us about it often, for much of that time we tried to laugh it off, or put it to the back of our minds because it was too bloody painful to contemplate. But Bernie knew this and that's why she tried to normalise it so often, forcing us to acknowledge our impending loss. That takes a special kind of bravery. I'll never forget her sitting us down, and she must have recognised our sadness and reluctance to talk about it because she tried to make jokes. She said, 'Right then, when I go, you can cry, a lot! But just for two weeks and then that's it, okay?' Of course, we joked back and laughed along with her, but the truth is, she knew how painful it would be for us all, and by her planning everything herself that she could, it did lessen the hurt a little. Another friend of mine also planned her own funeral in advance, and I tell you, it's a good job she did because her husband was in such a state that he could never have done it all by himself.

When I spoke about this with my friend and co-presenter Linda Robson she told me she'd not just thought about what she'd want for her funeral, but crucially, spoken to family about it. With Irish roots on her mother's side, she has memories stretching back to childhood of attending services – the first one being in Ireland when she was 7 and going to say farewell to her Nannie Ellen – a huge event, with cars and people everywhere. It's a common thread in so many cultures that funerals, burials, committals or memorials are community affairs – to support the living by honouring the dead. But for some people death is still their deepest superstition – as if by talking about it, you summon it closer. Really, though, there's a freedom in being able to talk about these things. Linda told me how she'd originally thought she'd prefer a traditional burial, but has changed her mind now to cremation – so her ashes can be turned into necklaces, meaning her children can always keep her with them. It can be hard having these conversations – but so special too. And yes, it's just as important to let our family know if our wishes change. I think we'd all want a day that reflects us – and I love that Linda hopes her send-off will feel like a celebration of life – complete with *Always Look On the Bright Side of Life* as one of the songs!

All of these different approaches show that there's definitely not a rulebook for facing your mortality. For some people, it's time to tick off the bucket list, and for others, it's an intensely private moment of contemplation. And of course there are some people who can't or won't accept that they are dying, or will tell the doctors that they'd rather not hear the prognosis. I've known people to not tell their nearest and dearest, or others to drop it into conversation like they're talking about where they're going on their holidays. There's no accounting for people's wishes. After all, if they don't want to talk about it, it's not an easy conversation to have one-sided. This happened to a friend of mine, stage performer Debbie McGee. Paul Daniels, her beloved husband, would absolutely not acknowledge that he was dying, even though Debbie suspected that he was fully aware of the fact, and she definitely knew. It was really painful for her having to hide her true feelings from her husband, because he was trying to live life as normal, even though it was about as far from normal as you can get. For people in Debbie's situation, it can mean they effectively start their grieving alone, even while their loved one is still alive.

'The doctors told me privately that Paul had around two months left to live, and that I had to decide where he would spend what time he had left,' Debbie told me. 'And of course I knew I would be bringing him home, so that's what I did, but I couldn't speak to him about any of his wishes. I couldn't even say goodbye to him, I just had to be really strong and face each day as it came.'

The tumour on Paul's brain was growing and affecting him more as time went on, but he was very bright, very intelligent, and was still able to enjoy the simple things, such as walking around the garden with Debbie, watching his favourite TV shows and having long evening chats just like normal, but never once did they speak about the inevitable.

'It was particularly hard for the family,' Debbie said. 'They all knew, of course, and wanted to come see him to say goodbye without ever saying it. They all did that in their own way, but never all together as they didn't want to overwhelm him.'

Debbie and the whole family had to discreetly plan everything while trying to keep things as happy for Paul as possible, and create as many memories with him as they could.

Advance planning for our funerals means that should the unimaginable happen – that we are taken suddenly – then we aren't leaving our loved ones to think about what we might like. A friend of mine had always assumed that her elderly parents would want a cremation. Most of their friends had been cremated, as had other family members. It was only a chance conversation with her dad that made her realise he wanted a full mass and burial.

'I was just sitting there, having a coffee with them,' she said, 'when an advert came on the telly about making a will.

The lady in the ad was saying she wanted a simple cremation and my mum said that's what she wanted, when Dad chirped up that he wanted the full monty. Catholic mass service, classic hymns and a burial. I was stunned! Fancy finding this out when your dad's almost bloody ninety!'

The thing is, talking about death, especially our own, just feels wrong somehow and we all tend to avoid it. I believe we should all try to normalise it by talking about it whenever we think about it, because let's face it, no matter how healthy we are, we all think about dying at some point. The other thing we could do, if we really don't want to enter into that discussion, is to write down our wishes for our funerals. Just the once, get it all written down. Which songs or hymns would you like? Do you want it to be a formal, black-wearing affair or something else? Where would you like it to be? Do you want a cremation or a burial? You might think that family members should know all this, but honestly, we don't.

Bradford GP and TV personality doctor Dr Amir Khan is a good friend of mine, and he had me laughing my socks off when he took part in one of my podcasts about funeral planning.

'I want curry at my funeral, of course,' he said. 'Ideally made by my mother if she's still around, and if not, she'd better leave the recipe somewhere safe!'

He explained that in their family they have huge funerals with five hundred-plus guests who all come to pay their respects and give condolences. There were over a thousand guests at his father's funeral. I told him I was quite jealous about that and that I probably didn't know five hundred people who'd want to attend mine.

'Oh, we all sit down to eat at the service,' he said, 'and there are always huge vats of curry for everyone to eat. I've also chosen the type of music I want playing – for me it's Nineties R & B. I want a sexy vibe going on, just like myself.' He laughed and then added, 'Listen, if people want to grind at my funeral, they can grind.'

Well, that's one funeral I want an invite to if I'm still around when it happens!

Jeannie Conroy from Co-op Funeralcare says that just in the last decade funeral services have changed so much, and people are much more likely now to have a very personal-ised service.

'Don't leave it too late,' she said. 'You can call in to have a chat with a funeral director at any point to plan your big day. It doesn't have to be formal – we can call to see you at home or even meet you in a café or somewhere. Wherever you'd feel most comfortable. We try to get to know you as much as we can and help you to tailor your service to some-thing that suits your personality.'

I asked Jeannie if there had been any really memorable services she'd officiated over during her years as a funeral director and she told me of one that had stayed with her.

'The lady had been a Zumba dance instructor for years,' she said, 'and planned the whole thing from start to finish with us. At the end of the service, when people usually stand and then walk out in line to a favourite hymn or song, the music started up and the whole congregation Zumba-danced their way out of there, all happy and smiling as they danced by the coffin and out the door. It was indeed very special, and a very fitting ending for that particular lady.'

Love Island contestant and UK Mental Health Ambassador Dr Alex George told me that he definitely wants to be cremated, but that he wants the service to be very relaxed.

'I do like a traditional service,' he said, 'but I want it to be kept very simple. Like, I'd like for all my family and friends to maybe go to a beach afterwards, and to picnic and drink while remembering me.'

I asked him what music he'd like to have playing at his service, and the little monkey said, 'Stayin' Alive!'

He was joking about that. At least, I think he was because he went on to say he'd like to go back to his teenage years with the choice of music, with perhaps some Nirvana and a bit of Elton John.

As these conversations show, there are so many ways of planning a funeral – traditional or contemporary, solemn or celebratory. You'll find so many options – from wicker caskets to committals at sea, woodland burials or having your ashes turned into diamonds! And trust me, as I found when I was speaking to the experts when I first started my podcast, funeral directors have heard all kinds of strange requests, so if there's something you want, don't be afraid to ask. From people wanting the *Star Wars* theme played at their funeral, to requesting guests do a Mexican Wave – it never hurts to ask!

As these conversations show, there are so many ways to structure a funeral – traditional or contemporary, solemn or celebratory. It can be an expensive process, and many people choose to start saving for it, to alleviate the pressure on their loved ones. But there are smaller, more private ways to do it too. You might have read about some public figures recently who've brought attention to 'direct cremations' like the one David Bowie chose – an unattended cremation was his choice, and a family memorial was held on a different occasion. Do what feels right to you – and your family and friends. Is it the comfort of a familiar church, is it a wild and beautiful place to scatter ashes, or is it a knees-up for people to swap stories?

One other thing that we tend not to think about when considering our affairs after we pass away is that almost everything we do these days is password protected: our online banking, our emails, our social media, files that we keep with our utility bills, credit cards, etc. Bestselling author Candice Brathwaite recalls that, after her father died, the family were in a real mess, unable to access his online affairs. She and her husband, as a result of that, now have what they call a 'death file' – a bit of a morbid name, I know, but still, what a brilliant idea! It contains all the passwords and file locations that either of them would need should the other die suddenly.

I've loved doing all my podcasts on advance planning as it's made me realise that I too should get a move on and do some of this for myself. It's not just for the elderly or for those who know they are dying, but for all of us. It's one of the last nice things we can do for our loved ones.

Before I go

To think this all will end is a sombre thought indeed,
But when I take that journey, I know I will be freed.
I'm not afraid of going for I've made my peace with death,
I'll just be sad to leave you all, when I face my final breath.

Don't cry for me before I'm gone, I know you'll do that after,
Instead let's say our fond goodbyes with memories and laughter.
I've made some plans and shared some wishes,
not to make you sad,
But to help you when I'm gone, so you remember all we had.

Some say it's hard to think about the end and
while I know that's true,
I've found a strength and clarity in thinking what I'll do.
And knowing that I've made a plan has left me feeling lighter,
And it's made the days we do have left feel just that little brighter.

Chapter 3

I'M NOT DEAD YET!

I HOPE YOU'LL forgive me calling this chapter by a funny name, but it brings a smile to my face when I remember elderly relatives reminding me that life is to be lived right up until the end. And why not take every opportunity to celebrate a life – perhaps even before time has run out? It's only recently I heard about the concept of living funerals, and yes, I know it sounds like a contradiction, but they've become a way for people with a terminal illness to mark their final months and share them with people who've mattered to them.

If it feels too much to manage, or even a little morbid, then why not try speaking to someone who works in this field? We're all familiar with the amazing professionals that see us into this world, and anyone can see what an important role a midwife plays. So perhaps it isn't surprising that as well as medics, religious leaders and funeral directors, there are also people whose calling it is to help you make the choices you want around your death. Death doulas, as are they're often called, are there if you want to have conversations you think might upset family or friends, or just want someone who can focus on supporting you rather than having to handle their own grief as well.

But if a living funeral sounds sombre, why not have something a little more unusual? Bestselling author, and a friend of mine, Sam Michaels – who also writes under the name of Kitty Neale – surprised everyone who knows her recently by throwing a 'going away' party for her beautiful mum, Brenda. Brenda Warren was actually the original writer behind the Kitty Neale name before handing over the baton to Sam a few years ago, but she was recently given a terminal cancer diagnosis.

'It was devastating,' Sam said, 'but Mum decided there and then that she didn't want to put me through a painful funeral service, so when I came up with the idea of a going-away party, she was immediately on board.'

'Oh wow!' I said. 'That must have been so tough for you.'

'Not really,' Sam said. 'Mum threw herself into helping organise things and I think it helped take her mind off her diagnosis for a bit. Honestly, our family are slightly bonkers and we find the funny side of any situation, even one as sad as this. Mum wanted to dress as an angel for the day – to practise! So, we made that happen. Together we found an outfit – complete with fluffy wings and halo – and she looked amazing! I know it's not for everyone, but it was just right for Mum and her sense of humour. My hubby even dressed as the Grim Reaper, and we played lots of inappropriate music too. "Spirit in the Sky", "Always Look on the Bright Side of Life" – we all had a proper giggle.'

'That takes a special kind of bravery,' I said, really impressed.

'I wanted it to be light-hearted,' Sam said. 'We got to do all the emotional stuff too – an opportunity for people to come and hug my mum and share memories with her. But the funny parts meant it felt unique. We even played pranks on the guests. I left some blank cards and a couple of pens in the dining room, and guests were asked to write something for Mum in them – which I'll give to her later. But one of the pens was a trick one that gave you a little electric shock when you opened it. It was an amazing time. I'm so pleased we made it a day to remember.'

I certainly had never heard of a party like this one before! 'What about your mum, Brenda?' I asked. 'Is she happy you did it?'

'She said she enjoyed every single moment of it, especially all the wonderful hugs she got. For me, seeing the outpouring of love for Mum, it was genuinely uplifting and so touching. If people have the time, as we had, I'd definitely suggest doing something like this. You can make it really personal. I'll never forget it, and neither will Mum or any of the guests.'

How many of us have been to a funeral and wished we'd had the chance to say all the lovely things we want to share about the departed to them while they were still here?

A party like this can be a great chance – or you could think about other alternatives. The writer, TV critic and poet Clive James received his terminal diagnosis ten years before his death, and as well as giving him both the spur and the opportunity to write some incredible poems (many of them funny as well as moving), it also gave people a chance to tell him how much they thought of him, and a fellow writer collected these thoughts and put them into a book for him. I hope he felt the love and admiration from those who knew him. And he certainly told people not to spend time writing his obituary, famously telling people to keep it to a single line! Of course, there were wonderful obits after he died, because, like so many of the traditions around passing, they're for the living as much as the dead.

But his famous good humour around his own imminent end got me thinking about how we're often afraid of being seen to joke about death – but if you've been through the devastating process of getting a terminal diagnosis, then I reckon that's your free pass to crack any joke you like. Other people might be afraid of making light of the situation – but that doesn't mean you can't!

There's a lot of delicate language around death, as we'll find throughout the book. I know lots of people have strong feelings around terms like 'bravery' and 'fighting' diseases. It can feel like a fight if you're facing a life-limiting illness, but I do understand why those who know a condition will take their life don't necessarily want to feel like they've lost a battle. In fact, I've been lucky enough to speak to lots of people who at the same time as recognising that sometimes it's just utter bad luck to get sick also see themselves as lucky, even in the depths of that diagnosis: lucky to have the chance to tell people how they feel, lucky to have people around them who love them. It takes an amazing strength and mindset to do that – and it often goes hand in hand with a 'seize the day' mentality, making the most of the limited time we all have.

These days, we're all much more familiar with the notion of 'bucket lists'. There was a time when it seemed shocking – years ago when people were afraid to talk about death, let alone to acknowledge that someone might want to put a wish list together for what they want to try, see or do before they 'kick the bucket'. But I think they can be special for two reasons. The first is that it helps make the most of the time you've got, and making the moments special even when the months or years are short means we stop thinking about time running out and really live for the present. The second is of course to make memories. If you've always wanted to see Disneyland, walk on the pitch of your favourite football club or go in a hot air balloon – then go for it.

But don't think bucket lists have to be grand! Not everyone wants to try skydiving or to go to Graceland, and lots of us might not have the health or money. But there might be little things that mean a lot – things you or your loved one want to try or even experience again. A lovely meal, a vase of favourite flowers – you can build a list of little moments of joy that can be just as special as daredevil adventures or far-flung trips.

'I think nowadays, people are more likely to admit to time being short, and are more open to embracing the days and letting go of things that have been holding us back. This can be true whether we're facing our own mortality or coping with the news about someone we love. Suddenly things we've always worried about feel trivial. Perhaps you've hated wearing a swimsuit on the beach – but who cares about what you're wearing if you just want to feel the sand between your toes or paddle in the waves? Sometimes approaching the end just has a way of making us focus on what matters.

I really like the movement these days to not save things for 'best'. We've all done it – saved fancy outfits, posh crockery or left our sparkliest shoes at the back of the cupboard – waiting for some occasion we think is special enough, and then that day never comes. So use your best bag, wear the heels, put your favourite lipstick on – because why shouldn't today be special?

Seize the day

Grab the good glasses
Open the wine
Use the best plates,
Now is the time.

Let's shout out the things
We used to once whisper,
Let's say everything
While time's on our side.

Tell me the stories,
Don't fear to smile,
Crack out the jokes,
Now is the time.

Don't be afraid to sit and
Tell me I'll be missed,
Don't be scared to laugh
At my wild bucket list.

I'm savouring each moment,
Not standing in line,
Treasuring each day,
Now is the time.

Chapter 4

THE FUNERAL

SOMEONE ONCE SAID to me 'the funeral isn't the worst day of your life, the worst is the silence after'. And while I think there's so much to unpack in that thought, which we'll come back to later, it does tell you a little bit about why all kinds of cultures and civilisations have had rituals, ceremonies and rites around death and bidding farewell for countless centuries. Like with grief, there's no right way to mark that final send-off, but whatever you're facing – a full production funeral or the briefest of official markers – it can be worth preparing yourself for how you and those around you might feel. I often think funerals are as much about those left behind as those who've died.

And when it's someone really dear to you, I can tell you that on the day of the funeral of your loved one, it may take every single ounce of courage and strength that you possess. Often you really are locked in your own grief at the funeral, so much so that you may fail to notice how much others might be hurting too. I remember feeling so angry at my sister Bernie's service. Yes, she'd planned it all herself, and yes, it was beautiful, but honestly, the platitudes and the number of times I was asked how I was – I just couldn't cope with it. I mean, how did they think I was feeling? I was acting out of the ordinary, that's for sure; it wasn't like me to be livid, but that's what grief does to you. It's completely normal to not feel or act like your usual self. I'm not saying it's a licence for bad behaviour, but people will understand if you're out of character.

I was feeling so bad around Bernie's funeral that I took to Twitter and posted:

I wanna run until my legs break, scream until I have no voice and cry until I cry blood. How's that for how I feel?

Some might think it was wrong of me to vent in public like that, but it was an outlet at least, and I needed it. I was so wrapped up in my own feelings, my memories, my guilt, my shock, that I didn't really have it in me to consider anyone else. Of course, I had my family all around me, we were all there for each other, and I did know they were hurting and suffering just as I was. My friend Candice Brathwaite said to me, 'the front row of a funeral hits different', and I know exactly what she meant by that. That row, the same row I've sat in so many times now, is a bubble of pure grief. The mourners in that row don't even try to remain stoic. Their pain is palpable and personal, loud and animalistic, and they cling to each other, searching for some kind of comfort.

Speaking with my friends from Cruse Bereavement Support and Co-op Funeralcare, I've learned that people preparing for a funeral tend to fall into two categories. The first are those who, like myself, try to keep busy, almost acting out a normal life, and those who don't even have the strength to get out of bed, who want to hide away from the world. Interestingly, both sets of people will give the same reason for behaving as they are: an attempt to put off the inevitable. I found similar themes came up in conversation in the podcasts too. It made me think that with all the losses I've suffered, I'm quite the pro these days. If someone were to ask me how to cope at a funeral, I think I'd say that preparation is probably key.

A funeral summons such a huge array of emotions that the littlest thing can feel like a mountain at the time, so don't leave anything until the last minute, and certainly not until the day itself if you can help it. Plan ahead what outfit you're going to wear and set it aside all ready to put on. Delegate whatever tasks you can to relatives and friends – it's too much for one person to take on. Make sure you eat breakfast that morning, and I know you won't feel like it, but it's important, so do try to manage a bit of something. If it's for a close family member, do make sure that you keep in regular contact with your funeral director. Trust me, you are not getting on their nerves, they don't think any question is silly, and they really are waiting for your call – it's what they are there for. They'll have seen and heard everything in their line of work. As the only people on the day who aren't grieving, they can be relied on to keep the practical side of things running smoothly. Remember too that services such as Cruse Bereavement are not only there for you after a funeral, but they can be called upon at any point during the process. If you are feeling overwhelmed, just give them a ring and they can talk you through any worries or feelings you might be having. Samaritans can also help you, so never think you have to deal with it alone; reach out, because they know just how you are feeling and really can help.

You might feel that you are the one expected to read or write a eulogy at the funeral of your loved one, and while some people are able to do this, others simply can't. They just know they will break down and have no control at all over their emotions. If this is you, then it's totally fine; you don't have to put yourself through that. You can write down in advance all the things you want to say and get someone else to do it for you. Don't feel guilty that you're in some way letting your loved one down, you are absolutely not. Don't forget, they knew you, they would know how hard it would be for you to stand there and read out a testament to their life, so don't burden yourself if you're not up to it. Instead, when you have a strong moment before the funeral, write down some of your best memories and say the things you'd like others to know and then hand it over to your funeral director. They will make sure it gets read out in the manner that you'd like. If there is humour in there, that's fine, you just need to capture the personality of your loved one. And do get input from others who knew them too so you don't feel any added pressure about making sure you get it right all on your own.

Of course, funerals are about more than words. I've known some people who aren't good with speeches but have played an instrument or chosen some beautiful music to say what we so often can't. In any service, there are likely to be people from many stages of a person's life – they might know them as friend or family, colleague or neighbour – and most of us find out other sides to a person in the readings and memories shared in a service. The nice little old lady next door might have had a wild rock-and-roll youth, or perhaps your quiet colleague from accounts was a weekend Hell's Angel and wants a heavy metal send-off. Because of that, it can be wonderfully up lifting to have a selection of words and music to show different sides of a life. But don't rule out the power of silence too – often a modern service invites the congregation to share a few minutes of quiet contemplation, and in this calm, everyone gets to say farewell in their own way.

We are such a jet-setting world right now, and a lot of families are scattered across the globe, or at least in different parts of the country; we often hear people saying that they only really get together these days at weddings and funerals. This is sad, but true. Just a couple of decades ago, extended families were often very close and lived near each other, but nowadays we are lucky if we know or see all of our cousins and aunts and uncles. This means of course that after a funeral there will often be a big get-together, a celebration of sorts – often referred to as the wake (although I know a lot of my Irish friends would think of the wake as the laying out before the funeral). After the sadness of the service, the mood can be lifted at the wake – a chance not just to share grief but also to chat and laugh with family and friends you may not have seen for years. I know this can be hard for some, as they may feel guilty about having fun at such a sad time. A friend of mine remembers being devastated after her nanna's funeral, and she couldn't believe it when she saw everyone laughing, drinking and joking in the pub afterwards.

'It was like a massive free-for-all party,' she said to me, 'and that day I hated them all. I thought they couldn't have possibly loved my nanna, not like I did, if they could forget her within the hour.'

But we know that's not how people feel, really. After a funeral, emotions are in overdrive, our bodies are tense as we try to control those emotions, and in order to get back to feeling okay we need an outlet. The wake or celebration of life afterwards is just such an outlet, and after bracing ourselves to get through the service, we can relax a little. And, of course, sharing happy memories is a powerful thing – a habit to learn to embrace rather than feeling we can't speak their name. I've never been to a funeral where I didn't learn something new about the person I've lost:

sometimes funny stories, often surprising glimpses of the person they were before I knew them, or even surprising requests they've made for their funeral. Whether they want no mourners or pina coladas all round at the 'afters', wake or no wake, it doesn't matter. What matters is that you do it your way, but there is no shame in giving your loved one a good send-off.

What a day to face

Oh, what a day to plan for,
What feelings it will bring,
What flowers should I order,
Who'll choose the hymns to sing?

Should it be quiet and solemn,
Or colourfully celebrate life?
To know you're gone forever,
It cuts me like a knife.

Yet I pull myself together,
There's so much left to do.
To come together in your honour,
With all who cared for you.

I know we need this moment,
A time to all draw near.
And when we share our memories,
I'll feel that you're still here.

Will the words I chose be fitting?
Will they share the best of you?
What a day to have to plan for,
What a thing to have to do.

Chapter 5

LIVING IN LIMBO

WE'VE TALKED ABOUT getting through the day of the funeral, but for me and for lots of people I know, the day itself isn't the hardest point, it's the days and weeks that follow. I was definitely living in limbo after my sister Bernie died; I just didn't know what I should be doing. Should I still be wearing my grief like a black armband so that everybody knew I was still hurting? Should I resume life as normal? I didn't know what was expected of me, or even what I was capable of. I realise now that whichever path I chose would have been the correct one, because at some point we have to carry on, right? Back then, though, in my confusion, I felt that nobody really understood what I was going through, the messages of condolences fizzled out, and this in turn made me want to avoid others. It turns out that this wasn't a problem at all because in fact I found that others were actively avoiding me.

I should have expected it perhaps. When I lost my mum, I witnessed people actually crossing the street to avoid talking to me after the funeral and the first few weeks. People simply don't know what to say after a period of time has passed. Is it too late to say they're sorry for your loss? Is it still too soon to say that? Will they bring up painful memories? The truth is, I'd have preferred that people just acknowledge it, and that they didn't feel awkward at all. It's more awkward in my opinion to act as though nothing has happened when it quite clearly has.

My friend and TV personality Jake Quickenden agrees, and admits that when he is approached by anyone actively avoiding the subject of his loss, he brings it up, often quite abruptly and uninvited.

'I'd rather it was spoken about,' he said. 'My dad and my brother are on my mind every single day, so I'm never going to act like they aren't.'

After his dad died, Jake dealt with the limbo period by trying to completely ignore his ongoing grief. He felt so guilty that he had left the hospital and gone home, missing the moment of death, that he couldn't face things.

'I surrounded myself with my mates,' Jake told me, 'and just partied and got drunk a lot. I did anything I could think of to supress my grief. I was too scared to stop, because I knew that if I did, I would be flooded with guilt and sadness, it was awful.'

Jake had just started processing the loss of his dad to cancer when only two years later, his 16-year-old brother, Oliver, was diagnosed with osteosarcoma, a tumour on his leg bone.

'Throughout his whole illness – when his hair fell out, when he had his leg removed and was in a wheelchair – he never once complained. Our Oliver, who loved sports, now had a titanium leg and could hardly do anything. He just shrugged it off.'

Young Oliver spent a long time fighting his illness but unfortunately, despite a short remission period, the cancer returned and this time it had spread throughout his body. Jake remembered not being there when his dad died and wanted to make sure he was around for his brother, so he spent as much time as he could with him.

'When the end came it almost broke me,' Jake said. 'I was round there one day, and he was just 19 years old, but he was bed-bound by now, and he looked at me and said, "mate, I can't do this any more, I've had enough." Me being me, I told him not to be stupid, and that he could still beat this thing, but I knew in my heart that he was done. Three weeks later he was gone. Thank God I made it to his bedside in time, though, because just before he died, he opened his eyes, took my hand and said, "I love you, man".'

Jake dealt with the period after Oliver's funeral completely differently. He didn't have to try to block out his emotions with booze and parties because his grief this time wasn't the same. He said he recognised how badly his mum was affected, and he had to be strong to support her. He was actually able to set his own grief aside while he helped her to deal with the loss of her young son.

'I use humour, a lot,' Jake admits. 'For example, if I'm with a new mate, someone who doesn't really know my past, they might say something like, "oh, what does your dad do?" I just go, "well, he just lies there really, doesn't move". Then when they're looking at me for further explanation, I go, "mate, he's dead!" And then of course I laugh at their reaction. One of my best mates lost his dad, and we both laugh and joke about it, like we'll call each other the "no-dad crew". It's just the way I deal with it now. I'm never going to avoid the subject or not talk about them.'

Jake's advice to anyone who doesn't know how to treat somebody who's grieving is to not even try to avoid the subject, don't feel awkward and treat the person exactly the same as you always have.

The truth is that during this limbo period your emotions will be all over the place, and while sometimes you'll want to talk about what you're going through, in a lot of cases you won't be in the mood for talking to others, and that's fine too. Indeed, sometimes it's a good thing you're not. A close friend of mine told me that she actually felt like smacking some people who had visited her during this time. She knew they were doing their best, trying to be supportive, but the seesaw emotions of mourning can be wild. Some people even have trigger phrases and platitudes, and for my friend it was being told 'he's in a better place now', and 'I know exactly how you feel'.

'Well, no, they bloody well didn't!' she said. 'Honestly, I felt like throwing them out of the house.'

It's true that nobody knows exactly how you feel because everybody grieves differently, and in the depths of loss, only the most devout of us feel our loved one is in a better place. The better place would be right here, with us. When people say things like this to you, it's not that they're uncaring, it's simply because they haven't experienced it themselves. Nobody has experienced *your* grief. The best we can do is try to acknowledge that our friends are doing what they can to show that they understand our pain – even if it's in their own way. Likewise, I know some friends who show their love in other ways – for some people, it's tea and sympathy, but other friends might lend their support by bringing round meals to make sure you've eaten, tempting you out to get some fresh air or even offering to walk the dog. Help comes in many forms.

Some people, during the time immediately after a funeral, believe that they should 'get away from it all', but sadly, packing a bag and going off somewhere can sometimes be just like packing your grief in the case. It will still be there, it goes wherever you go, and you have no choice but to face it eventually. Putting it off is only temporary; sooner or later it will bubble to the surface and find an outlet.

Debbie McGee remembers that she was in shock for almost a year after her husband, Paul, died. Shock is the body's way of protecting the mind, and it is essentially doing the task of setting your grief aside until your mind is able to deal with it.

'But before that, after my dad had died, I don't think I grieved properly at all,' Debbie said. 'In fact, almost eighteen months later, Paul and I were on a plane, flying back from somewhere, and suddenly, mid-flight, and for no reason I can understand, I just burst into floods of tears. To this day I don't know why that happened. Perhaps it was because I was flying home and the realisation had hit me that Dad wouldn't be there. I just don't know, it was very strange.'

But this is grief. It can hit you at any time, for no apparent reason. Despite the model of grief being numbered, our minds and bodies completely disregard this and will throw any one of the stages at us at any time, and especially in this limbo period. All we can really do is ride it out and realise that tomorrow will be different. Hell, the next hour might be different, and somehow we find the strength to get through it.

Another thing Debbie McGee told me, and I've never forgotten it, is that people say time heals. It doesn't, not really. The grief stays the same size, always, we just have to build a new life that is bigger than it.

From a Parent to a Child

I'm only just a dream away, I haven't truly gone,
You're my proudest legacy, you're how I go on.
And that way I'm still here with you, in your heart and mind,
In everything I taught you, to be brave and be kind.

You made me a parent, showed me a deeper love,
Some say I'm looking down on you from somewhere high above.
But I feel I'll stay nearer still, inside your very heart,
For life and death themselves can't pull our bond apart.

We were made so like each other – and not just DNA,
All our life experiences, our battles and our play,
Each thought and smile, each joke we shared,
I live on because I know you cared.

There is no sadness, no more pain, where I have gone away,
I'll walk in spirit with you, child, each step of every day.
The love we had, it does not go, it was too broad and deep,
And so I love you still even in my eternal sleep.

Chapter 6

MORE THAN
A FEELING

NATURALLY WHEN WE think of grief we think of it as an emotion, usually as something close to sorrow. But I think it's worth being honest here and saying that grief is more than how we feel. For most of us, grief will be a physical state too. It might be one that lasts a short while or manifests itself in bodily changes that stay with us or change us in the long term.

I think we're all familiar with some of the sensations that come with bad news – it might the racing heart of shock, the prickling of tears in our eyes, a lump in the throat or a heaviness that feels like we've been punched in the stomach. These are all intense physical reactions and ones that will pass after the initial moments. But I wanted to touch on some of the longer-lasting symptoms often experienced but far less often talked about.

A good friend of mine, Lou, had lost her husband of many decades to a heart attack. Our circle of acquaintances were all shocked and rallied around her, and while she seemed to be managing all the tricky admin around a funeral and even coping with living on her own, I felt there was something she wasn't sharing – even though she'd been amazingly honest about her emotional ups and downs.

'You're going to think I've gone mad,' Lou said when I finally found a way to ask her what she was going through. 'Sometimes I think I might be losing the plot myself,' she continued. 'You see, ever since Mark died, I've been getting chest pains. And I don't mean indigestion or bronchitis or any of the things I'd recognise. It's as if I'm having sympathy pains for Mark, as if I miss him so much my body is echoing his. I'm worried my heart is going to give out next. You see, I said you'd think I was going loopy!' she admitted.

'Not at all!' I replied. I'd heard a little bit about the idea of sympathy pains – although usually they're most commonly experienced by men supporting their pregnant partners in childbirth – and I know our bodies can be at least as mysterious as our minds. 'Have you been to the doctor?' I asked.

Lou told me she hadn't wanted to tell her GP how she was feeling, in case they felt she was wasting their time, but I encouraged her to chat to her doctor, and she was glad she did. They sent her off for a lot of tests, and while she was relieved to find there was no evidence of any heart problems, they did tell her that extreme stress like she'd been through could lead to palpitations and other tremors. 'Lou was given a course of beta blockers and some monitoring, and was told she'd done the right thing by going to the GP.'

'Do you know what surprised me the most?' Lou asked me a couple of months later, when she was feeling much better. 'I read up on what I'd been through and I'm so glad I did go for those tests. It turns out it's not just in books and films that you can die of a broken heart. It's called takotsubo cardiomyopathy and they're still researching it. But it made me realise everyone was right – it's always worth getting things checked out. There's often help available, if you can go and look for it.'

Lou's story has stayed with me and I realised lots of us have all kinds of strange symptoms during grief and feel too low or isolated to seek support. I've listed some of the common ones below.

Change in appetite: this can be either a loss of appetite or an incredible hunger. Your stress hormones will be all over the place, and, even if you don't want to, try to give your body the nourishment it needs and make sure you remember to drink. Take advantage of those cups of tea people might offer, and top up your water bottle.

Different sleep patterns: I've known night owls become insomniacs after losing someone, and equally I've had times when I've hardly been able to get myself out of bed I've felt so wiped out with grief. If your sleep is suffering, it can be hard to function, so while you shouldn't put any pressure on yourself to get a certain number of hours, do try to set up routines that give you the best chance of getting some rest. I know it's hard, but resist the urge to be on your phone last thing at night; give yourself some bedtime rituals – whether it's a few pages of a book or just some nice hand cream.

Panic attacks: These can come in many forms, and we might even confuse the symptoms with other conditions. If you find yourself struggling for breath, feeling dizzy or with chest pains, it could be a symptom of a panic attack, but it could also be something that requires urgent investigation, so do contact the professionals. And if after you get checked the doctors do tell you it was a panic attack, please don't let your friends or family write it off as 'just' a panic attack. It can be terrifying when you're in the middle of one, and yet with some education and preparation you can also find ways to identify, lessen or even prevent them.

These are just some most commonly reported physical symptoms, but I know from experience that there can be many others. Headaches often recur, along with sensitivity to noise. Many people experience memory issues after they've lost a loved one too – we can be in such a state of shock that our brains can find it very hard to form or access memories for a time. Most of us usually recover from this after the acute phase, but sometimes I wonder if the brain is trying to protect us by not letting us remember some things.

There are also some lesser-known ways our bodies can tell the story of loss too. Someone I met at work trusted me with their story of losing a very good friend in a road accident as a teenager. I've touched on how traumatic our first experiences of losing someone our own age can be, like with me and Linzie, and I don't think it's surprising that sometimes our bodies can express shock more easily than we can in our words or feelings. Ally told me how profoundly the death of her friend affected her at the time – not only did it make getting back to school and studying understandably extremely difficult, but she also found her hair started to thin and fall out. We've all heard of the notion of someone's hair turning white with shock, but actually hair loss, temporary or permanent can be an even more regular side-effect of shock and grief.

But what amazes me is not just how our bodies reflect our emotional states, but how resilient they can be. When we feel like we don't have the strength to go on, our bodies often prove us wrong until the mind catches up and we feel able to engage with life again. So, if you can, treat yourself with love and patience, and our wonderful bodies – in all their variety, young or old – will thank you for it.

More than a feeling

They say it hurts to be in love, that any love brings pain,
But what I feel since losing you, I'm sure I can't sustain.
My chest gets tight if I even speak your name,
And thinking that you're gone burns deeper than a flame.
I thought loss would be a feeling, a storm in my imagination,
But then came waves of hurt and physical sensation.
There's a ball of pain inside now, in this shell that once was me,
And as it grows, I wonder will I ever set it free?
They say the path of grief will finally lead to healing,
And the hurt, will that fade too? It's more than just a feeling.
Yet the thing that brings me hope, a small but shining light,
Is knowing that there still comes day after each night.
The sharpest pains can fade, and numbness wash away,
One day the words will come again for what I need to say.
When I was too sad to speak, my body did it for me,
Felt all my sorrow and just let it be.
So I'll give it time to heal, tread softly a little longer,
It's what you would have told me, and that's
what makes me stronger.

Chapter 7

THE ANGER

IN THE TRENCHES of grief, it's not unusual to have no words for how you feel – and in that sense of loss and bewilderment, to lean on the words of others. C. S. Lewis, alongside the Narnia books so many of us know and love, wrote movingly about mourning. You might have come across this powerful quote of his: 'I sat with my anger long enough until she told me her real name was grief', which captures a little of how our emotions can come piling up on us at a time of a loss, refusing to stay in neat little boxes.

But the angry stage of the grieving process is likely to hit us all eventually. No matter how calm a person you might usually be, no matter how placid you normally are, the anger after the loss of somebody close can consume you. Of course, death often leaves many understandable angers – the things said or unsaid, the feelings that run high around last wishes, funerals or that tough topic of wills and finances. But just as often the fury can burst into flame from the smallest spark. It doesn't always start with a little niggle of annoyance that builds up within, either – this anger can be triggered by absolutely anything and often appears out of the blue, immediate and sharp. How dare that couple be walking down the street holding hands? How dare those women be laughing and drinking coffee like they don't have a care in the world? The rage overwhelms us, the tears start, and then, *bam!* You're right back there at the start, drowning in your grief.

When I spoke to *Mrs Brown's Boys* actor Gary Hollywood, he shared how he lost his brother during the whole pandemic lockdown fiasco, and he believes that those challenging circumstances contributed to the intense anger he felt. He recalls trying to bottle up his feelings so as not to upset anybody else, and then having to go and scream into a towel in the bathroom.

'We had to move in with my parents when Gerard died,' he said, 'and then because lockdown happened, and the travel restrictions, we had to stay there, with a new baby too. There was just nowhere to hide. I felt like I had to stay strong for everyone else, and this made me so angry too.'

Gary's grief was made particularly hard because of the shock of Gerard's condition.

'He had been in hospital with Covid symptoms,' Gary explained, 'but then was given the all-clear, he didn't have the virus after all. Can you imagine our horror, then, when he died after having two heart attacks? He was only 50. And then of course to top it all, we couldn't even comfort each other at the funeral. It was all socially distanced. Terrible.'

I know that I turned against my faith. And coming from a religious background, as I did, this was no small thing. In fact I'd say I completely lost my faith in a God who would allow my mother to suffer as she had, who would allow my sister to die at such an age, who would steal away so many other beloved friends and family members. I raged at that God and then actively turned away from any thoughts of religion. For a lot of people, religion is a great comfort in a time of mourning – and the many rites and rituals of different faiths can help not just individuals but communities too. But for me, the pendulum swung the other way, and I found not just that I couldn't find comfort in my old beliefs, but that they were making me angry. You start questioning what you might have done to deserve such heartbreak. Mad with yourself, furious at others. You may wonder why, and what you've done to deserve the loss, ask whether you weren't a good enough partner, mother or father, or even that you're being punished for something you have or haven't done. It's natural to hit out at what feels like the unfairness of loss – to look for reasons when sometimes the hardest answer to hear is that often, there are no good reasons when it comes to bereavement.

What we need to understand is that this type of anger frequently manifests as a control-seeking behaviour. When we feel powerless, doing anything can feel like a victory – even getting mad. It allows us to temporarily impact our environment by venting aggression to overcome the helplessness we feel. It's a defence mechanism, really, but because each of us experiences grief in a unique way, it leaves us prone to doing things we wouldn't normally do. My friend Jake turned to alcohol to try to keep control of his emotions; others might turn to drugs, or start smoking, anything to quell the feelings of distress. At a time when rational thinking can go out of the window, it's really important to find some time to acknowledge the real reasons behind the anger.

If I were to try to describe grief-anger, I think I'd say it's like being trapped in a goldfish bowl that someone has shaken, like being tossed and twisted, damaged and broken. Filled with rage and countless other unregulated emotions, we want to be seen, and at the same time we want to give in and drown in our hostile environment. We want to scream out to be saved, yet we don't want to reach out. That requires effort and bravery, and it can also require us to let go of the anger. In the stormy seas of grief we often aren't ready to do that, so we remain in our goldfish bowl of pain, knowing we can be seen, yet not seen, and all the while, the world around us continues as though nothing is wrong.

I find the key to getting over this stage of your grief is to be completely honest with yourself and to analyse the real reasons behind your anger. I mean, you're not really angry at that woman sitting on the park bench who just smiled lovingly at her husband as he passed her a latte, you know you're not. The truth is that it's a very deep-rooted, primal reaction, a part of us that we can normally keep hidden. What we are truly angry about is the fact that she has something that we don't. We feel cheated, stolen from, and we want to be able to smile, happily, as she just did. We want someone to be around, to care enough to bring us a latte, and it's not bloody fair. Not nice to admit, but this selfish side of us has always been there, it's a kind of self-preservation, but as toddlers we're taught that it's not socially acceptable to display it, so we all learn to push it away and keep it hidden. Grief, though, won't allow for us hiding anything; it blows the lid off any suppressed emotions. Sometimes even ones we didn't realise we had.

Once we admit to ourselves that our anger is really all about us and not the rest of the world, we can start to work out how to deal with it. Some people choose not to, of course; we probably all know someone who suffered a loss many years ago and has never smiled since, and the thing is, maybe that works for them. Maybe for that person, living with grief and anger is the only way to keep their loved one in their thoughts. The choice is ours to make, however, and if we can just be brave enough to accept that, actually, we can find a way to live with our loss, then we can start to make progress. It is not easy, let me tell you; it's bloody hard letting go of that anger, and some days you will think, sod it, I want to be mad! But telling yourself every day that you will be okay and forcing yourself to get up and do something, however small, really helps. Plus, who's to say that you can't do both – scream into the laundry, glare at the ducks on the lake as you take a walk? Just find a little way to keep going.

A friend of mine, Karen, lost her teenage son in tragic circumstances (I talk about this more in a later chapter), and three years down the line she was able to admit to me the intense anger she'd carried for a long time.

'I can't believe it now, looking back,' she said, 'but I swear, Coleen, I couldn't leave the house for months and months because of the horrible thoughts I was having. I'd see groups of teenagers hanging out or just messing about round the shops, and my immediate thoughts were, how come they get to live? It was awful.'

It might have been awful, but it's also perfectly understandable because the pain she'd suffered had been unimaginable. I asked her if all that had gone now, or were there still moments even now when she felt like that.

'Oh, it never completely goes,' she said, smiling sadly, 'but it gets less. I mean, I can still bump into a friend who has a boy the same age as my Daniel would have been, and I find myself starting with the "why me?" all over again. It's just that these days I can shake myself out of it.'

So, how do we shake ourselves out of it? Well, alongside what my own experience has taught me, and everything I've learned in conversation with experts and professionals, and also of course with my own friends and family, it seems there are practical things we can all do that will help, and the trick is to do them regularly, even if at first it seems pointless, because the more we do them, the more it becomes our new normal.

The first thing you should know is that it's perfectly fine to talk to the person you've lost. No, you haven't lost your mind, it's normal, and many of us do it. Hell, you can scream at them to vent your anger if you wish – just make sure you're alone when you do this, of course, otherwise some might believe you have actually lost your mind. Talking to them out loud can help you to rationalise that, although they have gone, it's okay if you still feel their presence.

Talk more to others about your loss if you can too. They may not want to bring up the subject in case it upsets you, but there's no reason why you can't do it. Explain your anger to them and allow them to tell you it's justified, because simply saying it out loud to someone is often enough to start healing. Take a long walk to clear your head – even if it's to go somewhere out of the way so you can scream at the heavens. This helps, and it beats punching a pillow because, well, it's a walk, a great form of exercise, so win–win in my opinion.

Another thing the professionals advise is to take up something new, something creative perhaps that will allow you to express yourself in the way you want, such as painting, sketching or writing. A different outlet for your energy, your emotions, your anger is something new for your brain to focus on, perhaps without painful links to the past. There are bound to be clubs and classes in your area, and they love to welcome newbies. You could take up yoga, or Zumba or dancing – anything that sparks your interest and gives you a challenge to fill that void. From pottery to poetry, there's some kind of physical or creative outlet there for everyone. Even if you are convinced that it won't work for you, because you're half right, nothing will magically take away your loss and feelings of grief, it might just help balance those feelings. So give it a try and tell yourself initially that it's just something you will do to pass the time, to get through another day or evening. Give whatever you pick at least three attempts, and if by then you're not enjoying it, or getting anything out of it, then leave, and try something else. One of the strangely liberating parts of grief is the sensation that you've faced some of the worst things life can throw at you – so you might worry less about smaller things like taking up a new hobby or challenge. The worst that can happen is that you've tried something new. The best that could happen is that you find you love it, you excel at it and you might even make new friends. Now, how can that hurt?

This Anger

I'm angry at the whole damn world, I need to scream and shout,
Once I had an inner light, and now it's all stamped out.
Endless days and lonely nights, cut through with silent screams,
Cravings for a chance of sleep, so I can see you in my dreams.

It's the only place you visit me, my mind, alone, at night,
The dark is all we share now, I miss your love and light.
It's hard to wake, to leave you, another day to face,
But when the anger fades, love still takes its place.

Chapter 8

ALL THE FIRSTS

THE 'FIRSTS' CAN be particularly painful for some people. By that I don't just mean the birthdays, the Christmases and the anniversary of losing someone, but all the other occasions and routines too. I personally can't take it in my stride as some can. When it's the anniversary of Bernie's death, or even her birthday, I tend to shut myself off. Other family members put little memorial posts up on their Facebook or Instagram accounts, but I won't go on social media, and I definitely won't be writing a tribute on that day. It's just too hard for me, and besides that, I think about Bernie every single day, so I don't want to only commemorate her on these even more difficult anniversaries, I just can't do it. But that's the thing – even in one family, we all grieve differently, we all remember her in different ways. Some people cope by boxing off their feelings and only letting them out on anniversaries; others can only get through those anniversaries by not acknowledging their feelings. For me, though, it's like she's always with me anyway, forever only a thought away.

But as I said, it's not always the 'big' days that are the hardest to navigate. I often think it's those firsts that you least expect which hit you the hardest. I remember talking to a good friend of mine who'd lost her husband, and she was telling me that the first time she looked out of the bedroom window and saw snow after he'd died, she got all excited and immediately turned to tell him, but of course he wasn't there.

'It hit me like a ton of bricks,' she said. 'I thought I'd been through the worst of it, and then six months later, that happened, and suddenly it was like day one all over again, sobbing my eyes out, gasping for breath, and feeling very sorry for myself.'

There are so many instances like this, ones you never think about as significant before you encounter them, before something catches you off guard. I've heard widowed friends tell me about the times they've made two cups of tea automatically, before bursting into tears when they remember they only need the one, now. Or the real challenge of learning to cook for one, when so much of the food we buy says 'serves two' on the packaging. Yes, it's the little things that can get you when you least expect it. There are so many times I've read or heard a funny joke, and I'll have a little giggle and think, oh, Bernie will laugh at this, and then I feel guilty, as if I'd momentarily forgotten they'd died. There's no need for that guilt, though. I know this, and there will come a time when those little memories are a comfort rather than a trigger.

I remember speaking with a friend in the music business about this, and he recalled a time not long after his wife had died.

'I knew doing things alone was going to be hard. When you've been married as long as we had, your spouse is just always there for big things and small. Suddenly, you have to ask people to come to things, or face them solo. The first time I had to go and perform without her I thought I was going to be sick. I couldn't imagine her not being in the wings.'

I suppose those red-letter days are occasions that anyone would suspect are hard – having to start afresh without the person you're mourning, or finding it hard to let go of the rhythms and rituals you shared – but there are so many other surprising moments that can catch you off guard and make you wobble that you just wouldn't think about until it happens to you. Another friend told me that what she found the hardest was the first time she was writing out a birthday card to her son, and instead of the usual 'love from Mum and Dad', she had to sign it just 'from Mum'.

'I sobbed my heart out,' she said. 'I couldn't bear it, and told myself there and then that I wouldn't do it, and I didn't. It was about two years before I could bring myself to accept that I was no longer half of a couple and could just put my name alone on cards. And then of course it hit me that from now on I'd only ever receive Christmas cards addressed to me alone.'

There will always be times that catch us unaware, and we can't prevent that, but we can put things in place for the big things, the things we know will definitely come, and also think ahead for some of the practical challenges we might face. What were the jobs our loved ones used to do for us? The things we did together? There are some places or routines you might want to avoid – and that's okay if it's your choice; it can be good to shake up routines and try something new. But equally, if there's something you need to go through alone that you used to do together, it can't hurt to do a little visualisation first, a few deep breaths, even confide in a friend that you need a boost. And remember, nothing's ever as hard as the first time. You might even surprise yourself in what you can accomplish. I have a friend who'd never driven on a motorway – her husband had always been the default driver. A couple of years on from her bereavement, she's taking road trips across the USA.

But holidays and trips out can often be difficult, and you may find that you really can't bear to go to the same places you enjoyed with your loved one. Some people will want to go back to a place where they shared special memories with their partner – it may help them to feel close to them. Others will want to give old haunts a wide berth and for them it is all about creating new memories. Never forgetting, but living differently. Always remember that your grief, and your way of dealing with it, is unique. My advice, at least for the first time or two, would be to take a friend or a family member on your first holiday without your loved one, and rather than go off for a week or a fortnight, just try a few days away to see how you cope. New horizons can be a wonderful thing, or you can feel at sea without your familiar routines and surroundings. Dip your toe in the water and see what brings you peace.

The first big celebration without your loved one, no matter who it is you've lost, is bound to be difficult. Whether it's Eid or Christmas, Hannukah or Holi, so many festivals are built on time shared with family and friends. It might be an opportunity to feel supported by the people that love you best, but so many people have told me that it can be one of the hardest times of the year too, and you may find that you simply want to shut yourself away from the world and be on your own. If this is what you need, then do it, but please, still make sure that you plan something to do that day that will nourish you, because even in your deep sadness, you need to allow your mind and body some respite from the grief. Order a good book and set it aside to read that day. Rather than tinsel, turkey and the trimmings, perhaps you could buy in advance all the things you need to make your favourite meal or make a plan of the things you will watch on TV that day. Make it all about you for once, and indulge yourself. Of course, none of this will spare you from the memories that come flooding back, uninvited, or the painful acceptance of your situation, but treating yourself with kindness makes it more bearable. Don't feel, though, that you have to stick to your plan, because you don't. If at some point in the day you decide to go for a walk, or visit or phone a friend, then do it, just go with your feelings, minute by minute, listen to what you need.

And if you do want to spend the holidays with friends or family, please don't worry that your presence will bring them down. It absolutely won't. They wouldn't invite you were that the case! Your friends and family know what you're going through and will want to help in any way they can, so allow them to. Children don't understand grief in the same way adults do, and can seesaw between sadness and joy, as the permanence of loss is hard for them to grasp – after all, it's hard enough for grown-ups to come to terms with. But please don't feel guilty if you are able to share in their joy and laugh at their happiness; it doesn't mean that you have 'moved on' or 'already forgotten' who you're mourning, it simply means that you are able to experience emotions other than sadness, and this is a good thing. Grief is full of contradictory emotions – I don't think I'd really grasped how I could feel so much at once until I was faced with bereavement. It is also worth a mention here that on days such as these, others will likely avoid mentioning your loved one for fear of upsetting you. So don't be afraid to mention them first. I often feel mentioning their name can be like breaking a spell, giving others permission to speak about your loss.

I spoke to someone recently widowed who approached me while I was researching this book and he shared some of the particular 'firsts' that stuck in his mind, and I was surprised by what he told me.

'My partner and I played in a band. Nothing professional – more of a hobby that we used to do with a group of friends. We met up most weeks and after I lost my Suze, they were keen to support me, kept inviting me, but I couldn't face it. The thought of being back in that back room of the pub we always went to, looking at the place she used to stand made me feel like I was going to faint.'

'Did you ever go back?' I asked.

'I did,' he told me. 'At first I said I was just going to go and watch, and you know, it was really hard, and I did feel like I was going to faint. But I didn't. We were all really sad that first night, we toasted her memory and then after that each time got a little easier, and in the end, I found I could sing again.'

It's important to remember that your 'firsts' are not anyone else's, so don't be upset if your friends don't always remember that it's their birthday, or a special anniversary. It's not that they don't care, it's just that you are the one who has these dates deeply ingrained, not them. However, if you need some support on those days, there's nothing wrong with reaching out and telling your friends that today would have been your fortieth wedding anniversary, or that you're really missing your mum on Mother's Day, or that today, the baby you lost would have been starting school. You'll be surprised that those friends can help you in so many ways. Just a long chat over a coffee or a glass of wine, sharing memories and feelings, can make all the difference. You never know, they may even share some of their own secret 'firsts' they have had to tackle too.

And if you don't feel you can reach out to someone to help you? Then you can also take the bold and generous step of helping someone else. There is a lot of research and evidence out there that proves giving is hugely beneficial on the most difficult days. I don't mean the giving of something physical, but of your time, your skills or just your compassion. If you can find a cause in your local area that could do with a helping hand, consider volunteering with them on the special days that are hard to cope with. The psychological benefits are massive and evidence suggests that voluntary work can even improve your overall health.

Those firsts will always be hard, but as the name suggests, the 'firsts' only happen once, and it does get easier. Time and tears are great healers. As people often say, time doesn't take the memories or the sorrow away, but you grow around it, through it and with it.

The First Time

I went to our bench the other day,
The very first time since you went away.
I looked at the sky as I ate fish and chips,
Remembered the time you wiped salt from my lips.

I so wanted to turn and see you there,
For you to steal a chip, ask me to share.
I smiled, through my sadness, the first time this week,
Saw the irony as I wiped salty tears from my cheek.

The empty space beside me was echoed by the sky,
But the memories bloomed as the clouds went by.
The next time I visit our bench I'll be stronger,
I will smile and know I can stay a bit longer.

Chapter 9

THE ACCEPTANCE

As I said right at the start, this word 'acceptance' is one I've found hard to understand. The very idea that we must accept the fact that life will never be the same again is just too huge to come to terms with easily, and I guess that's why it sits way down at the bottom of the grief model. I think we can only approach acceptance when we change the definition. We aren't accepting that their passing was okay by us, and we aren't accepting that they're gone and now we must move on. What we are actually accepting is that our life will continue without them, but that it will be a different life and we must learn how to live it without them.

I asked my friend Debbie McGee how she coped with this, and she told me that in fact this was the most important stage of her grief, and that actually she only started to move forward with her life after speaking with a friend of hers, who also happened to be a grief counsellor.

'I was talking to him about the physical pain in my gut,' she said, 'that I just knew was a big ball of grief pain, and I asked him, does this ever go? He smiled at me and told me that no, unless I changed things it wouldn't go. He said, "what you have to do is create a new life around that pain and it must be bigger than it. Only then will it crush that physical ball of hurt, and then, Debbie, it won't come back".'

I've thought about that a lot since speaking with her, and it makes a kind of sense to me. The pain after losing someone close is physical, but you can't just pop a couple of paracetamols for that type of hurt, can you? No, that friend of Debbie's was right: it's down to us to build something bigger than our pain so that it pales in significance. Don't get me wrong, it never goes completely. We probably all know someone who keeps a bottle of their mum's favourite perfume, because scent is so evocative, while another widowed friend of mine wears her husband's watch to keep him always near. Some people can't bear the reminders but for others they are an ongoing comfort and all of this proves that even after the acceptance, we still keep their memories alive and very much still a part of our lives.

Debbie McGee chose to take on different things in her career in order to move forward. Challenging herself to do new things as one person and not as part of a couple was a brave thing to do because she had built her career alongside her husband, and it's taken great strength.

People often say marriage is a partnership, and of course we focus on the emotional devastation when you lose a spouse, but it would be naïve not to mention how for many people, losing a partner also means losing professional or financial security. Some people are fortunate enough to have saved or have insurance if the worst happens, but for many people, losing a husband or wife can mean losing half the household income, and if you also work together, it can mean the very way you make a living has to halt or change. It can take time to work out what to do next or how to do it, but that's entirely normal.

It shows that there is no stopwatch ticking away when it comes to mourning. And even when the most acute parts of grief last for months without turning into that kind of deeper, quieter grief many of us learn to live with, it can still heal, improve or simply change. I think that's one theme I've noticed when dealing with the aftershocks of losing someone: however you feel now, it will change. Sometimes for the worse, sometimes for the better – but the waves will keep coming and slowly you can learn to float with them rather than let them crash over you and knock you underwater.

Bestselling author Candice Brathwaite lost her dad when she was just 20 years old, and one of her children was born on the anniversary of his death. She says she was afraid that because of that, she'd never be able to properly move on. I asked her did she ever question whether perhaps her child was a kind of gift from her dad. That can be the strength of family ties – even when generations don't get the chance to meet each other, connections can echo down through the years, joining us together.

'I kind of did, eventually,' she admitted, 'but it's still bittersweet when birthdays come up, et cetera, but I have learned to live with it and accept it. You know, you just see things differently when something like this happens. And you have to move on for the sake of those left behind. I can talk about my dad all the time now, and both of my children speak of him as if they knew him.'

Candice also admitted that the difficulties she faced, trying to come to terms with the loss of her dad, were the main reason she wanted to have more than one child. She told me that her grief had almost killed her, and she had no siblings on her dad's side to turn to.

'I was adamant with my husband that I couldn't just stop at one child,' she said, 'because I never wanted them to have to go through what I had. I needed at least one more child so that they'd always have each other to turn to in tough times.'

When I was speaking to funeral care professionals about moving on and acceptance, Andy from Co-op said: 'We often find that learning to live with the grief we experience involves not ceasing the relationship with the person who has died, but working out ways in which we can remember and cherish them, and carry these memories with us as we go about our lives. As human beings, we are wired for attachment and connection with those we love and we feel safe with.'

He's right of course – it's all about finding the right balance. The loss of a loved one will almost certainly have an impact (no matter how you felt about that person – and yes, it can be complicated), but there are things we can do, steps we can take to make the process that bit easier, and it's all about what works for you.

I've written already about trying something new, about being kind to yourself and about taking things a day at a time. But while you try to look after your mental health, it's important to look after your physical health too. I'm not talking about tying on your trainers and planning a marathon (though I've known many people who do find running a great way to relieve stress or even to fundraise in someone's memory) – no, I'm talking about the basics. Think about your houseplants – they can't grow without a bit of water and a bit of sunshine, and nor can you.

When I've been in the throes of grief, or a close friend has, I turn to a very basic checklist. When you're clearheaded it might seem really simple, but from the depths of grief these little acts of self-care are often the things that fall away. I asked a friend who was struggling to go through the following with me:

Have you had a drink? Fill up that water bottle or let a friend put the kettle on.

Have you eaten something? Even if you don't feel hungry, try something plain just to give your body and brain some fuel.

Have you had a shower? Or if that feels too much, a soak in the bath or a splash of water to your face can sometimes be the literal refresh you need.

Have you been outside? Fresh air is a great way to blow the cobwebs away. And if you can't manage a walk, then how about you just aim to sit outside and look at the sky for a while – even an open window can be restorative.

If you can tick these things off your list, even as you mourn, then you should be proud that you're taking small steps even when it feels like you've lost your way.

And when even these actions feel like too much to manage, try to build little routines so you don't have to think about them. Creating a routine can have a powerful impact on our ability to heal. It helps create a sense of order at a time when our emotions are all over the place. Whether it's waking up at the same time every day or taking the dog out for a walk, sticking to a routine helps us feel grounded, and it can help our brains run on autopilot while we process the big things we're going through.

Remember that support comes in different shapes and sizes too. If asking a friend or family member feels too hard, or you simply feel too alone, there are so many organisations who can advise on professional help. If you can't reach that elusive acceptance yourself, you might benefit from a guide along that road.

That last one, about support, is quite interesting. Support can come in many forms. I spoke with someone who volunteers as a grief companion while I was researching this book, and she told me how she'd formerly worked as a teacher, and had taught a young boy who'd lost his mum at a tragically young age. She met with the child every week for eighteen months, and in all that time he always changed the subject whenever his mother's name was mentioned, until the day he left primary school and the tears came. He'd finally found a way to express his grief, and all those quiet sessions had done their work supporting him up to that moment where he could let go. He might not have had an outlet for his grief until that moment, but having that safe, trusted time and space with a teacher meant he knew he wasn't alone.

And that's the thing, isn't it? It's so easy to feel like it's just us going through it, even when we know it's not. And it's the same with processing grief, finding acceptance or moving forward. Long, long after the funeral, when everyone else appears to have got their lives together and forgotten all about it, there we are, still deciding whether or not to get out of bed on a morning! It's hard to resist the temptation to compare our own inner thoughts and struggles with other people's outer appearances – we might just not see they're struggling in their own way.

Then you wake up one day and don't immediately think about them and you feel that actually, you *can* cope. The hurt is subsiding. You decide that from this day, you will start to live again. It's all going great until one of those 'firsts' we explored earlier comes and startles you, and you're back where you started. Yes, you can experience this stage of acceptance many times before it is really the right time. Acceptance, really, is learning to let go of trying to control what we are experiencing, and embracing the fact that feelings will come and go, but that we are more than just our feelings. It can be incredibly liberating when this finally happens, and we realise that yes, we can get through the darkest hours and that dawn will come again.

Half of me

I remember feeling whole once, before you came along,
But then our two lone melodies mixed to make one song.
Together we made sense, and you made me complete,
We had it all then, you and I, the whole world at our feet.

But now you're gone, I'm half again, and I don't know how to heal,
I need you to rebuild me, to how I used to feel.
I want to hear your voice again, to feel safe in your embrace,
I need to feel your touch again, I need to see your face.

One day will I be whole again? I know acceptance is the key,
But for now, my love, I'll carry on, and just be half of me.

Chapter 10

THE TRIGGERS

WE ALL KNOW that after a relationship breakup or a divorce there seem to be happy, smiling, even kissing couples everywhere you turn, just everywhere. In restaurants, on the street, in the park, on TV; it's like the universe is laughing at you and showing you what you no longer have. Well, it can be the same after a death, and often even more so, because it's not always a partner you have lost, it could be a parent or a sibling. Just when you're feeling at your most alone, everyone else seems to have something to celebrate. You might be watching your favourite soap when, lo and behold, the storyline is packed with happy families. The news headlines even seem geared to highlight what you've lost, and social media is reminding you that it's Mother's Day or Father's Day, or national blooming sister's week or something.

The truth is that in fact the universe isn't playing tricks on you, the whole world isn't mocking you, it's just your grief going into overdrive. Under normal circumstances you wouldn't even notice these triggers, you wouldn't notice that loved-up couple walking past you, but right now you are searching for answers still, seeing signs and symbols everywhere and you need to find reasons for your pain. Your brain reacts by saying 'stare at that image [or sign/ trigger?], that will make you cry, that will validate your feelings and give you some release'.

Reminiscing over memories or looking at old pictures is another way that your brain allows you to have a little weep now and let out some of the pent-up emotion. But it's worth remembering that these days memories can crop up more easily; it's not always a case of getting a photo album out – thanks to social media you can just pick up your phone and get confronted by memoires you weren't expecting. But you know, eventually, those same photographs or social media memories that set the tears flowing now will start to have a comforting effect on you, and cause you to smile when you see them. In the early stages of grief, you'd be forgiven for wanting to tell the next person who tells you to 'be grateful for all the happy times you had' to put a sock in it. But in time, memories come to bear more sweetness than sting – even if they will always be slightly bittersweet.

There are lots of other triggers that might trip you up unexpectedly, and you can't really prepare for these. Such as when you see someone who looks like your loved one, or you hear of someone with the same name, even the same job. You might meet someone who shares the same love of music or food or favourite colour; all of these things are enough to spark a memory, and then out of nowhere, the feelings erupt once again.

I remember about a year after my sister Bernie had died. I was sitting in my car at the traffic lights, humming along to whatever was playing on the radio, and I suddenly smiled and thought, oh! I must ring Bernie and remind her about this. The song had triggered a memory of something, I can't recall what, but then it hit me, I think for the very first time, that she wasn't here any more, and in fact I'd never be able to talk to her ever again! I burst out crying at those traffic lights as I allowed myself that realisation, because prior to that I'd always told myself, she's not really gone, she's living in Surrey, and I don't see that much of her anyhow. I think in times of deep grief our brains allow us to tell ourselves anything in order to keep the pain at bay, but the brain can't filter out these unexpected triggers. Looking back at my moment I suppose it's a good thing, really, because it got slightly easier for me after that, and it does help with acceptance.

When I was in my mid twenties I had a friend who'd just had a baby boy, born with feeding and breathing difficulties. After a few weeks in hospital, and after learning how to tube feed him, she was able to take him home and she was so happy. That little boy fought for his life, through all kinds of illness, but sadly, at just four months, he died. I couldn't comprehend how awful that was for my friend and I felt devastated for her. Eventually she moved away as she couldn't bear to walk the same streets she'd pushed her pram around, and it was almost ten years before I saw her again. It was a random meeting in Sainsbury's, I think, and she told me she was paying a flying visit to her sister. We went for a coffee and a catch-up, and before long we were laughing and chatting together like old times, but I kept noticing that she was constantly glancing across to another table.

'Do you know them?' I asked as I followed her gaze.

'No,' she said with a sad smile, 'and you're going to think I'm daft after all these years, but every now and again I hear a baby cry and it sounds exactly like Michael. It's silly, I know, but every single time that happens it bloody yanks me right back to that day.'

When I'd bumped into her, because I hadn't seen her for so long, I too had remembered straight away about little baby Michael, but it had certainly never occurred to me that after ten years my friend would still feel that raw pain at the sound of a baby's cry. It's so terribly sad. How can you avoid a trigger like that? The experts at Cruse Bereavement and Co-op Funeralcare tell us that actually we can't avoid it, and we shouldn't really try to. Maybe very early on if we find it too difficult to face, then yes, we can avoid places that trigger painful memories, but down the line they advise that we should try to face them head-on in order to get past them and make life a bit easier for ourselves.

A great example of this came from another dear friend who had lost her husband when she was only in her fifties.

They had holidayed together in Menorca for years and it was a place she loved dearly that held such special memories for her.

'The kids had been pestering me for two years to get back out there,' she told me, 'and I kept telling them that I couldn't, not without their dad.'

In the end, her children's persistence paid off and her daughter bought her a holiday for Christmas.

'It was one of those flipping singles holidays too,' my friend told me, 'and I really didn't want to, but in the end, last year, I bit the bullet and just went. I was so scared on that plane, and I remember telling myself that if I hated it, if it made me too sad, I would just jump on the next flight and come home.'

She didn't fly home, and in fact admitted that she had a really good time.

'I met a couple of new friends,' she said. 'Both widows like me, and yes I had to walk into the same bars I had with Gordon, and pass the same tat shops on the harbour that he used to laugh at, but it was strangely comforting rather than being painful, and the memories it triggered were nice ones.'

So nice in fact that she and her two new widow pals are planning a trip back there!

The death of others can be a painful trigger too. We all remember the day Princess Diana died, and the day of her funeral too. There was such an outpouring of public grief, just as there was more recently when our late Queen died, and I know so many people who were reminded on both of these occasions of their own lost loved ones. We cry at such occasions even though we didn't know them personally, because when we've suffered a huge loss ourselves, we are either transported back to our own loss, or we empathise with the ones left behind. I mean, who can fail to remember the sad picture of young princes William and Harry looking so lost and confused, walking behind the car that would carry their mother on her final journey? It was heartbreaking, and I think we were all triggered in some way as we witnessed that.

So many of us find it hard to think about death, and it's often easier to think we're immortal than face the inevitable – but we do that all the more with those in the public eye, as if their fame protects them. But I'm old enough to remember when Elvis died! The reaction of the world was unbelievable. I often think about why I cried that day – sobbed my heart out is more accurate – because at that time I hadn't suffered any close bereavements that I can think of, and yet I grieved for a pop star I barely knew. So why? I'm sure now that the reason that so many 11-, 12-, 13-year-olds cried that day is because it was the first time they had seen such shared shock and grief. I can remember parents, grandparents and neighbours all in tears or disbelief, whole neighbourhoods came outside, stunned at what they were hearing on the news and wanting some-body to tell them it wasn't true. Now, over forty years later, a lot of my generation still remember the date that Elvis died.

So many children are marked by their first experience of grief – whether after a natural disaster, an atrocity or just a terrible accident. But when it comes to reported deaths, often it's the loss of an individual that affects us the most – perhaps it's that we can connect to that one single story as a real person, that beyond the statistics and headlines, we feel that human impulse to mourn a loss. It can be hard, but don't be afraid to let children share their feelings about loss with you. And who knows, sometimes it can even break the tension, as they often are brave enough to say the things we cannot, ask the questions that leave us tongue-tied.

The Triggers of my Grief

I hear a voice that sounds like you and it takes my breath away,
I turn on my car radio and hear a tune you liked to play.
So many little things these days can catch me by surprise,
A joke, a film, a jewel the colour of your eyes.

No one else would know the cobbled street where
you once fell down,
Or that every Friday afternoon, we'd meet for coffee in the town.
But these are things that trigger me, things others just don't see,
It's not just anniversaries, at least it's not for me.

It's waking on a summer's day and wishing you were here,
It's putting coins in a collection tin for a cause you once held dear.
One day I think it will hurt less, and that is my belief,
But until then I'll learn to live with the triggers of my grief.

Chapter 11

DARK TIMES

'THE BLACK DOG', as many people call depression, is something that's as personal and varied as grief itself. Depression can hit at any time, for many reasons (or indeed, for none), but when it's caused by grief, it's a particular kind. I think it's worth jumping in here and saying often when we go through a bereavement, we respond in line with our personalities – if you're usually introspective, you might deal with it by withdrawing into yourself more; if you're a natural-born drama queen, then you might want to mourn more publicly. As I keep saying: there's no right or wrong to it. But when it comes to depression, it can creep up on you in the most out-of-character ways. It can leave the chattiest of us lost for words, the social ones among us turning down every invitation, and it can hollow out those who other people usually turn to for strength. And it can come at any time – immediately after your loss or sometimes even years later.

After my sister Bernie died and the funeral was all over, people went back to their normal lives, yet I was still so depressed. I didn't want to get out of bed, I didn't want to go out, even to work, and I felt as though I'd never get out of the pit I was drowning in. Then one day I suddenly remembered those words of Bernie's: 'When I'm gone, Coleen, I'll allow you two weeks. For two weeks, you can cry, a lot! But after that, you get off your backside and you carry on. Get back out there.'

Daft as it sounds, that memory is what finally spurred me into action. I forced myself to give my head a shake and got back out there, just as my sister wanted me to do. I mean, obviously it wasn't as easy as that, it was baby steps and I still had many bad days, but it was the start of my recovery. I didn't have the strength to do it for myself – but I could do it for her.

Sadness like I experienced is entirely natural after a death. But I think we're often afraid to look at those points where it becomes more than sadness. Because depression is such a big term, spanning tough but manageable periods of mental health and mood problems right up to crippling mental struggles that make an semblance of normal life impossible, I think we can be wary of knowing where we or a loved one might be on the spectrum from sorrow to moderate depression to a mental health crisis that can involve suicidal thoughts. When someone close to me experienced what is called complicated or complex grief I had to learn a lot about what that meant. Complicated grief disorder, not often diagnosed here in the UK, is when intense, long-lasting symptoms of grief, together with ongoing problems and the inability to cope with life, go on for more than six months after someone you love has died. It's not normally diagnosed because it's difficult to identify. Almost all of us experience some symptoms of depression to a degree after suffering a loss – and sadness is natural at a time of mourning, but do watch out for it becoming a more widespread or all-encompassing sorrow. One of the key differences, according to experts, is the length of time we feel this way, and after weeks or months of being unable to function properly, we may need to reach out for professional help.

We can all offer support to friends and family, or if we're experiencing complex grief we can read up on the symptoms and treatment – but if you or someone you know is finding life unbearable, it is really worth reaching out and engaging with trained support. It can take some time to find the therapist or counsellor that suits you – don't give up if you don't find the perfect fit on first attempt. When you do find the right person to speak to, it can change everything.

You might feel that existence is pointless without them, and that feeling can be intense and overwhelming, feelings can and do change. Your actions don't have to be governed by your feelings – you can choose to put a little space between you and your feelings, to accept that your thoughts and actions are as much a part of you as your emotions, and you can sit tight and let the hardest feelings pass.

I've spoken to people who even thought they would welcome death so they could reunite with their loved one, and people who thought that everyone else would be better off if they weren't here. We shouldn't be afraid of these thoughts, but we don't need to think them alone. We can get through these moments – we just need to find a way that works for us

These days people often turn to social media to express their dark thoughts. At first, you might find lots of people respond saying they are there for you, but as it goes on, fewer responses come – after all, it's not the most personal and private of forums, even if it's one of the most accessible, and people whose only outlet is online report reaching a stage where they feel others don't really care. Do remember that online life is not real life – it's a brilliant way of connecting with people far away or if you can't get out and about, but if you can, reach out to people in person or on the phone too. If you feel that friends have fallen away – people who say they are there, but the phone calls have stopped, the invitations have stopped, and you feel you that you are a burden now – just remember there are other places to talk to people too, other organisations to call.

And if people are quiet, it's often not because they don't care, but because words can be hard to find. This is because in fact nobody understands the enormity of grief unless they've experienced it for themselves, and even then it's not the same, because as I've said, we all grieve differently. The truth is that if we were to reach out, simply tell a friend we are struggling and need help, then they'd be there for us, but it can be easy to convince ourselves that this would be pointless. But when it comes to the point that we are no longer taking care of ourselves, nourishing ourselves or doing simple things like shopping for groceries, we have to admit that we are in fact in the grip of depression and we need some intervention.

The experts at Cruse have identified certain risk factors which almost certainly add to the likelihood of complicated grief:

- How the person died: if they died in a sudden or traumatic way, this can affect how we grieve.
- Your relationship with the person who died: if you were estranged from the person who died, or had a big falling out with them, this will affect how you process your grief.
- Family conflicts: existing family conflicts, or memories of difficult childhood conflicts can also have an impact on the way we grieve.
- Loss of a child: if you have lost a child, you will be far more likely to be affected by complex/complicated grief.
- Previous bereavements or multiple losses: if you've experienced other deaths in your past, especially in your early years, this can make complicated grief more likely.

- Grief overload can hit you if you lose other things around the same time as losing a loved one, such as your job, your home or a divorce.
- Existing mental health conditions: this will obviously have an impact on how you grieve and can leave you prone to complicated grief.

Just reading this list shows you how many factors might be at play, how many different reasons there might be for one person's bereavement to be so very different from another's. But while we might all feel our sorrow differently, we're all deserving of help when we need it. No one's giving you a score for how serious your grief is, no one's expecting you to justify a need for support, intervention or just human contact. So please do pick up the phone, knock on that door, or send that text.

When Linda decided at the last minute to reach out to the mental health crisis team, help was swift.

These kinds of acute crises can need rapid intervention – but they can sometimes pass quickly too. Similarly, you might feel you have (or even have been diagnosed with) mild depression – but if it lasts long enough to be deemed a chronic illness, it can be exhausting. Don't feel you need your depression to be at a certain level before you it merits treatment. The bravest thing you can do is start talking.

While it can be hard to find the words to talk about depression and suicide, there are so many campaigns these days to help fight the stigma that can surround mental health issues. I'm so pleased that everyone from sports people to the royal family have spoken about how important it is to be able to tell someone when you're struggling.

Nowadays, most of us will have had some experience of mental health struggles ourselves or know a friend or family member who's been affected. And as we get better at talking about it, it also means there are more treatment types than ever before. Because our state of mind during grief can be so personal, it's no surprise that finding a path towards feeling better should be just as individual. From medication to CBT, exercise regimes geared to boosting your mood or hypnotherapy, there are endless routes to try. Of course, none of these methods will be a complete cure, and one friend told me while I was deep in grief that whatever I tried, it would at least keep my mind occupied while time worked the real magic not to heal my grief, but lessen the sting.

Another one of my plain-speaking friends told me she found going to group therapy really helpful – and not just because speaking to strangers about her pain was liberating, but also because she was convinced her day to day friends had done enough mopping up of her tears, even though we said we were always there for her.

So, how do we help ourselves or someone else who is suffering from depression after a loss? The big thing, for the more serious type of depression, is to get the right professional help. Start with your GP if you are able to do that, but if you genuinely feel on the brink, then it's probably better that you contact a specialist such as Samaritans or one of the bereavement services who can guide you to the right people for your particular need. You might need to be prescribed antidepressants, and despite some of the negative press, these really can help both short and long term if necessary.

I said earlier that words can be hard to find when you're reaching out for support, so don't feel afraid of leaning on other words – poems, books and songs can mean so much at hard times. Of course, silence can be healing too. I know one friend who swears by music as a healer, and another friend who found that meditation apps give her the peace she needed to find. Above all, take something or someone with you on your healing journey. A friend or a song, a verse or a book, it helps you feel you're not alone. Even the act of letting time pass in safe, non-judgemental company can show you that even the most powerful of emotions change, and while the hardest moments may be some of the ones that shape you, they pass, and there will always be new things around the corner – even when you can't lift your eyes to the horizon.

I Can't Go On

Without you there is nothing, only darkness, tears and sorrow,
Who would actually care if I don't wake up tomorrow?
Without you I'm a burden, hurting others with my pain,
I know that they're all thinking, *oh! Not this again!*

Is there a place where you are waiting? Would I join you if I die?
I know I'd hurt my loved ones, I tell myself and cry.
I can't go on without you, yet you always thought I could,
You deserve me to be stronger, just like I said I would.

In time I'll find some inner strength, I'll do it just for you,
I'll get the help I know I need, and I'll speak about you too.
But if for now I feel I can't go on, I'll just be, until I'm right,
Then soon I swear to you, my precious love, I will get up and fight.

Chapter 12

THE GUILT

GUILT IS ONE of the emotions that can overwhelm you at any time, and for a multitude of reasons. Perhaps you're having unrealistic thoughts about how you could have prevented the loss. Maybe you feel you should have listened more carefully when they were talking about their health in the past? Maybe you wish you had insisted they went to the doctor sooner than they did? Perhaps you regret not pointing out how bad the weather was that night they took that final car journey? The truth is it's more than likely that you couldn't have prevented anything, and when you have the time to really examine your thoughts, you will realise this. Some people feel guilty that they chose to not visit a dying relative; perhaps their life was too busy at the time, or perhaps they couldn't bear to see their loved one at the end of their life. Whatever the reason, it is usually cause for regret when it's too late.

The thing to remember about guilt is that this emotion is usually a burden we put on ourselves. Others would never want to subject us to it, especially when they see us drowning in our grief, but we do it to ourselves, almost as if to punish ourselves for still being around when our loved one isn't. We look back over events that unfolded before our loved one died, and we imagine how things might have gone differently. We torture ourselves with 'what if' scenarios, and at the time, we genuinely believe that we could possibly have changed the outcome. Later, of course, we eventually learn to accept that there was nothing we could have done to prevent the death. The loss won't be any less because of the realisation, but we at least stop feeling guilty about it.

One lady I spoke to who had lost her elderly mother remembers feeling acute guilt simply because of something she'd said a week before her mother had died.

'I was the only family member who could visit every day,' she said. 'My siblings all had very busy lives, jobs, and families to deal with, whereas I only had my husband to take care of and he worked all day. I never resented having to go every day – I'd done it since Dad died two years earlier – but it was just some of the things Mum would say to me.'

She explained that she would often turn up and her mum would be in a bad mood and she would shout and take it out on her daughter. There was never any particular trigger, it seemed, and one minute she might have been smiling and laughing, but then it was if a switch had been flipped.

'I know she was in pain, and often got confused,' she told me, 'and I usually just put up with it, but that particular day it really got to me, and she said something about my sister being a lot more patient than I am. I got really petty, and I think I said something along the lines of "well maybe she should come visit you more often then, instead of it being me, every day". I felt awful afterwards, but then she died a few days later and for months I could not get that day out of my brain. I never told anyone what I'd said for about two years, I think, and I carried that horrible guilt with me for all that time.'

The lady went on to explain that the person she eventually told was her sister, and that she wished now that she'd spoken to her right at the start because it was only after that conversation, when her sister laughed it off and told her she was being silly, that the guilt finally lifted, and she was able to let it go and move on.

'She even admitted that she'd also been carrying a lot of guilt because she felt she'd left Mum's care to me for so long. It was good for us both, I think, to finally open up about our feelings,' she said. 'It brought us closer together too at a time when we definitely both needed it.'

I knew what she meant. As irrational as it seems, looking back, it's perfectly reasonable at the time. I still sometimes feel guilty now, when I'm thinking about Bernie. I'll think, oh, I should have gone to that show she invited me to, or, I should have made time to go see her when I knew she was feeling particularly low that day. I do know, of course, that were Bernie still here, she'd tell me not to be silly, and that

I shouldn't feel that way at all, but still, it's there, after all this time.

Just when you think that guilt has eased – the guilt you felt after an actual death – you then learn that you can be hit by guilt for almost anything, at any time, sometimes even years after the event. A lot of people have spoken about 'happiness guilt', and this comes from a variety of events. One that never occurred to me before was that after losing a close loved one, the birth of a baby, for example, becomes a bittersweet experience, rather than the really happy occasion it used to be.

'I looked at my new granddaughter,' one man told me, 'and she was so beautiful and perfect, but all I could think about was that my wife wasn't here to witness this. She adored babies, especially our own grandchildren, and it just didn't feel the same for me. Of course I loved the little tot, and I was so happy to be holding her, but at the same time I felt this terrible sadness that she'd never meet her grandma, and would never know how it felt to be loved by her.'

This is a common theme I've found, and is perfectly understandable. We've spent years, after all, sharing these special moments with our loved one, and then suddenly there's this void. Something great happens and you might turn to tell your loved one, or pick up the phone to call them, then you remember they are not there, and you feel that there's no longer any point in finding the beauty in anything. The thing is, this will also pass. It might pass like a flipping kidney stone, but it will pass. There will come a time when you can take pleasure again in a new grandchild, a family wedding, or an achievement. You do eventually learn that you can share your happiness with other people, your friends, your wider family, your work colleagues, and not just that one special person you lost.

Often, people find they feel guilty simply because they find themselves smiling or laughing, and they realise they haven't thought about their loved one for a few days or even a few hours. I remember being on a night out when one of our group, who'd been widowed for years by this point, got chatting to the bar lady. At the end of his shift she came and gave him her number and as she walked away he turned to me and shook his head, telling me how guilty he felt. He looked down at his hand and realised he'd forgotten to put his wedding ring on that day and said it felt like he'd betrayed the memory of his wife. Luckily he was surrounded by friends all ready to tell him he'd done nothing wrong. Guilt has no reasoning, it creeps up on us when we least expect it, and we need to work hard to tell ourselves it is simply a normal emotion that we are allowing ourselves to feel.

A lot of people actively try to withdraw from happiness for fear of betraying their loved ones. They may feel that others will see them being happy and assume they have forgotten they are meant to be grieving. This is another form of guilt that serves no purpose, and if we really thought about it, we would admit that our lost loved one would want us to be happy and would hate to see us in the constant state of limbo that grief leaves us in. Some people retreat from their ordinary lives because they know their sadness is having an impact on everyone else, and this causes them to feel guilty. In the TV series *After Life*, the main character says 'just because you're unhappy doesn't mean you have to make everyone else miserable', and although this sounds harsh, it's actually how a lot of people feel, and this is quite normal. There are people out there who really can't cope with the misery of others, and they will cut you short or avoid you, but always remember that there are far more people who love you, and will stick around for as long as it takes, no matter how sad you are feeling.

And then there's the guilt that some people feel about making any changes within the home. I've known friends who immediately cleared out the homes of their elderly parents, for example, because it was too painful to see reminders of them everywhere, or they might have emptied their deceased partner's wardrobe straight after the funeral. But then there are others – my family included – who took absolutely ages before they could throw away or donate so much as a jumper. They couldn't stand to part with anything for months, and even years! When a neighbour of mine lost her husband a few years ago, I got to know her daughter, Angie, who had started to visit her mum more often. She would sit with her for hours and encourage her to eat and just keep going, and she would do her shopping for her. We would stop to chat now and again at our local supermarket. I'd always ask how her mum was doing, and if there was anything I could do to help.

'I just can't get her to allow us to redecorate the living room,' she told me on this particular day, 'it's bloody awful! My dad was a smoker, and the ceiling and walls are still all stained with nicotine. All we want to do is repaint it or something, but she's being so bloody stubborn!'

'Maybe she wants to hang on to that,' I said. 'It might be comforting to still have those smells and that discoloured paintwork that remind her of your dad. I imagine it must annoy the hell out of you, but for her it's probably something she needs to hang on to for a while longer.'

'That's exactly what Mum said,' Angie replied, 'but it's been three years!'

I had to smile at that, because I've known some people who've spent decades keeping their house like a museum.

That's the thing about grief and guilt: they go hand in hand and have no respect for time. While some people may want to change things in the home, or even move house, because things as they were hold too many painful memories, others can't bear to change anything and may feel guilty even washing the last clothes that their loved one wore. Whichever way works best for you is the best way. There is no right or wrong way, it all depends on when you are ready. Only then will that void start to close, and you'll know that you're starting to heal.

Guilt

I am with you in those moments when your heart is filled with pride,
I have watched you feel uplifted, saw those happy tears you cried.
That you can still find happiness, without my being there,
Means more to me than anything, it means that you still care.

Do not feel guilty now I'm not there, I want to see you living,
Grab every ounce of joy you can, be happy, be forgiving.
Above all else, forgive yourself, for daring to have fun,
For me, for you, for everyone, catch every ray of sun.

Chapter 13

THE WORST KIND OF HURT

THERE ARE NO league tables of grief, no hierarchy of mourning. But I think most of us would agree one of the hardest bereavements to even think of, let alone experience, is the loss of a child. Those who have faced it say the agony of losing a child, at any age, is unparalleled. I think many of us feel deep in our bones that it goes against the laws of nature for a child to die before a parent, and as such, no sense can ever be made of it. But because of that sense of how grievous a loss it is, those who have to endure it are often left feeling even more alone because people are so lost for what to say, how to understand it, how to help someone in that most intense of sorrows. There are, though, so many more people who have experienced this deep hurt than is often imagined. I know for many people this chapter may be hard to read – and don't feel you need to turn to it if you're not ready – but I want people to know that these words are here, whether you've gone through such a loss or are looking to support someone else who's walked that path, and to know that there are people out there who will both acknowledge and share your pain.

Whether you lose a child before you even got to meet them, or have to say farewell to them in young life or old, it will always feel like a part of you has been lost with them. People who lost a child thirty or forty years ago, or more, still relive that day as if it were yesterday; they attest that it's a whole different kind of pain that never fades, though they find ways to bear it. Some describe it as the feeling of losing an actual physical part of themselves. There can be an emptiness and an absence that feels more powerful than any presence. You grieve not only their loss but the loss of their future and all the things you were supposed to be part of – the first day at school, their wedding perhaps, or them having their own babies. Life will never be the same again, and while it will go on for you, it is okay to acknowledge how different your life will be without them. It is the imprint of love.

One lady I interviewed when writing this book, Shirley, had lost her baby boy just twelve hours after he'd been born. Shirley, who is in her eighties now, recalled: 'He was one of the thalidomide babies. He was born with missing limbs and other complications, but they kept me asleep for all the hours he lived, and only woke me up after they'd taken him away and they told me he'd died. I've never got over it, never, and never will. It was horrible that I never got to hold him or tell him how much he was wanted and loved, and all these years later, I mourn him on his birthday, which was also the day he passed.'

It was also a time when people were reluctant to acknowledge how deep a scar losing a child can leave. Shirley spoke about how the platitudes she received at the time – 'it was for the best' and 'you're young enough to start again' – hurt her deeply and she still feels that hurt today, sixty-three years later.

'I'll never forget,' she said, 'after I'd been sent home from the hospital and told I needed a couple of days bed rest. My local doctor came to see me and gave me a bottle of sleeping tablets as I couldn't sleep and spent all day and night crying for my lost baby. He sat on the bottom of my bed and apologised to me. I don't know to this day why he said he was sorry,' Shirley said, 'but he followed it up with an assurance that I could try again, and that my baby boy was in a better place. I felt like screaming that no he wasn't, the better place would be alive and with me.'

I found it so powerful that all these years later the pain was still so raw, and while none of us can ever experience someone's else grief, I felt her pain so strongly, even as I admired her strength for carrying on. Shirley made me realise that even though any loss can come back and hit you, sometimes years later, the grief after losing a child really is never-ending. Future children, or existing children keep on reminding you, and have you wondering what your lost child might have looked like at a certain age, or how they might have done at school or college. When friends have babies, with all the good will in the world, there is always that tinge of sadness about what might have been.

Cruse Bereavement Support talk about the loss of your role. Parenthood is such an important part of your identity that to lose a child is like pulling a rug from beneath you. The shock is just incredible, even if you've been told to prepare for it, and you genuinely don't know how you'll ever go on without them. A lot of parents I've spoken to who've suffered such a loss have admitted that in that moment they wanted to die too. The ache, the void, was too deep to even describe, and they felt the only way out was to leave this life. It is a valid response – but please know it's one that passes. Don't be scared by the intensity of your feelings, but know that the tide always goes out again, eventually, after a wave breaks. The death of a child brings with it the most complicated of emotions – alongside the sorrow and anger there is often unjustified parental guilt too, for the fact that they have outlived their child.

Another lady I spoke to, Margot, had lost her teenage son two years ago, and during our conversation she kept breaking down in tears. There is often a really fine line between wanting to talk about your much-loved child, wanting to share their story and celebrate their life, and the effort it can take to say things out loud, as if by speaking things you make it real again. For Margot, she was still unable to quite believe that Sam was no longer with her, and having the conversation meant exploring that hurt again, even while thinking of her beloved boy.

'He was no angel, my Sam,' she said, 'and had in fact got in with a bad crowd of lads in our area, forever getting into trouble with the police and at school. He drove me mad at times, if I'm honest, but that one stupid day, and that one stupid choice, and he was gone, just like that. Each morning I wake up and curse that I haven't died in my sleep. I'll never get over it, never.'

Sam and his friends – all around 14 and 15 – had gone out one night and had been drinking cider. One of the lads decided it was a good idea to steal a car and go joyriding – a term I'll never understand. The worst thing possible happened that night and the driver, a 14-year-old boy, crashed the car, instantly killing himself and Sam, who was in the passenger seat.

'I just knew when the police came that night that it was different,' Margot said. 'It was a policeman and a police-woman who knocked us up, and my heart sank immediately. It was the look on their faces. I just knew this wasn't a visit to tell me that Sam had been up to mischief again. I just knew. I started screaming as the words sank in, and I couldn't bring myself to go identify my baby boy, I had to send my husband. They left me, numb and feeling like I was in a bad dream, with the female police officer, and a doctor was called I think, to sedate me.'

Margot said that her whole life has changed while griev-ing for her son: her relationship with her husband, with her other children and her friends.

'I'm not me any more,' she tried to explain, 'and often I just can't be bothered trying to make people understand. My husband still actually laughs sometimes! I can't imagine that. My other kids cried of course, especially at the funeral, but after that, for them, life went back to a new kind of normal. I don't have one other friend who has lost a child, so none of them have a clue how I'm feeling, so I just lock myself away in the house.'

Margot has finally taken the first step to helping herself though. It's early days, but she plucked up the courage to ring Samaritans when she was seriously thinking about suicide, and they signposted her to Child Bereavement UK.

'It's not a solution,' she said, 'and I thought it would be a waste of time, but they are helping me. Who knows if I'll eventually get better. I'll never forget, and I know the hurt will always be there. Yet just to be able to talk to someone who doesn't feel bad about upsetting me, who can say his name, that's helping.'

So, what do the experts advise on coping with the loss of a child? I spoke to many organisations, and while everyone will have a different story, the advice is often similar. Most organisations point out that it's vital to talk to others, to reach out to those around you, but it is especially helpful to speak with other bereaved parents. There are loads of groups and online forums, and all of the bereavement services can put you in touch with others who know what you are going through.

Another important piece of advice is to stay connected to your child as much as you can, no matter what age they were when they passed. I'm pleased to say that these days our amazing NHS staff are trained to help parents through baby loss and can offer the kind of support that Shirley never had all those years back. There has also recently been a new national policy which means that if you lose your baby before twenty-four weeks, you can apply for an official baby loss certificate. For some parents, that recognition of their child is a huge part of the healing process. I know of many grieving parents who have been helped by their hospital teams to make precious memories with their angel babies, and while they might not have a lifetime of moments ahead with their precious child, where possible they are given the chance to make some important memories to show how much that baby was loved. It's a powerful thing to remember that love isn't about the time you get to spend with them, and if that time is short, your love can still last a lifetime.

A particular sorrow around baby loss is that many expectant parents go through this at exactly the same time as many of their friends and relatives are also getting pregnant. I knew a friend whose daughter had been through something similar and she said was kind enough to share her experience.

'I've always had two best friends,' she told me. 'And we've always spent lots of time together – we've been on holiday together, been each other's bridesmaids, shared many a night out and all live close to one another. We have known one another since school so we've shared all sorts. Other friends have come and gone but the three of us have shared many, many milestones, happy and sad. One of the milestones that should have been joyful was when I found out I was pregnant with my first baby. I told both my friends and they were absolutely delighted about it. When we met up while I was pregnant, one of them said that she, too, had some news, and she was pregnant. Then our other friend laughed out loud and announced that she was also pregnant! We were so excited that our babies would all be born within a few months of each other!

As our baby bumps grew, we talked excitedly about our three babies and how maybe they would be the next generation of best friends.

I felt really good during pregnancy but one of my friends said she felt unwell from the moment she found out she was expecting. As our pregnancies went on, she seemed to feel worse and worse and was worried about the baby. Her scans showed that the baby was small, but nothing otherwise.

Then one day, several months in, she went for a scan which showed no heartbeat. She had experienced a missed miscarriage, which is where the baby has died but there have been no other signs. She was understandably devastated.

As well as grief to handle, there was the added complication of her two best friends having babies around her due date. She did still ask about our pregnancies, but I tried very hard to be aware that she might feel mixed emotions around the time of my baby's birth.

I made a note of her baby's due date and sent some flowers to make sure she knew that I hadn't forgotten about her. When my baby arrived, she was one of my first visitors, and despite her feeling sad about her own miscarriage, she still has a lovely relationship today with my little one and my friend's baby.'

Whether you lost your child young or later in life, when you feel able to, a memory box is a great idea and is a lovely thing to reach for and look through when you want to feel near them. Fill a box with treasured items, such as photographs, baby socks, a lock of hair, or if they were older, their wallet or purse, a piece of jewellery or a bottle of perfume – anything that reminds you of them. The box itself can be anything, decorated by you or a specifically bought box or jar even, but do keep it somewhere accessible, even if it's not in direct sight. You want to be able to reach for it whenever you need it.

Other ways of staying connected include talking to your child, in your head or out loud, it doesn't matter, just say what you feel and imagine what they'd say back. It really does help, and I know this because I speak to my sister all the time. A lot of people find journaling helpful too. You could write down any special memories, even funny ones to look back on whenever you feel like it, or write down things you'd like to say to them. Write your feelings down too. If you're feeling particularly angry or sad one day, write it down just as you're feeling it – this can help you acknowledge and express your emotions.

The most important piece of advice, in my opinion, is to reach out for help when you need it. Tell people what you need and don't need. You will find, particularly when it comes to child loss, that others don't want to bring up your child for fear of upsetting you, but if you want to speak about your child, tell people, it's fine. On the other hand, if someone is bringing it up and you aren't ready for it, just ask if you could change the subject as you're having a bad day. People will always understand and want to be led by you. Be honest with your family and friends about how you are really feeling; you might be surprised by their reactions, and the help they can offer you.

Finding the strength to look after yourself is vital too. You might not want to eat, or go out, but putting one foot in front of the other is a wonderful thing. Don't tell yourself you need to walk for miles, but tell yourself you're just going to take a few steps, and see if that leads to a few more. If you can't face going far, why not just look up – the wide blue sky or the dark mysteries of a starlit night can be soothing precisely because it is one thing that brings us all together. There will be someone else under that sky who knows how you're feeling, and it can remind us that light follows dark.

When you're feeling strong enough, looking out as well as up can help. The professionals talk about how we often forget that even though we are the parent, other family members are grieving too. One example given from the Sue Ryder organisation was of a young mother who'd lost her baby girl at just three months old, and who was so upset because her own mother couldn't discuss her feelings.

'She shuts me down every time I speak about it,' the girl said, 'and she's my mum, I need her!'

It emerged that the grandmother was so distraught at the loss of her granddaughter that she couldn't bear to even speak her name. She was aware that her own daughter was also traumatised but she felt she couldn't help her as she was too lost in her own grief. We really do forget when we are drowning in sorrow that we're not the only ones, and it's so difficult to get our heads around the idea that anyone else could possibly be hurting like we are. This is one of those times when you need your whole tribe around you – if your family are bearing the same weight of grief, reach out to friends or contact the professional support organisations. If you're a person of faith, speak to your worship leader, or if you're not religious, there are people out there to support you whether you consider yourself a humanist, atheist or don't even know how you feel.

It is understandable to get lost in your grief in an extreme circumstance like this. But know that one day you will find a path through. The thought that I come back to is that life shouldn't be measured in years, but in moments. If we lose someone young, they weren't loved any less. If we have to say goodbye early and we didn't get to watch them go through all life's milestones, their presence, their life still made a lifetime's worth of difference to us.

The Lost Child

I'm only just a dream away, I haven't truly left,
I know how much you're hurting, and how you feel bereft.
But I'm still here with you, in your heart and in your mind,
Those memories, that surge of love, that feather you might find.

I'm only just a dream away, please don't feel that guilt,
Think of how you loved me, the plans for me you built.
You do not have to say goodbye, you need not let me go,
Forever close in spirit, because you loved me so.

I'm the whisper as you lie in bed, the rustle in the trees,
I'm the shapes you see within the clouds, that change
with every breeze.
I'm the feeling of contentment, I'm in a warm embrace,
I'm with you every moment that puts a smile upon your face.

I'm only just a dream away, we don't have to say goodbye,
Your tears have been enough now, please no longer cry.
I'm your child forever, and until we meet again,
I'm resting with the angels, no sadness and no pain.

Chapter 14

THE LONG GOODBYE

WE ALL KNOW that life and death are two sides of the same coin – and for most of us, that's how we make our way through life, knowing that death is inevitable but also that it's out of sight. How then do we cope if we have to live life with the end in sight?

Getting diagnosed with a life-limiting disease or condition is hard to absorb, and we've all watched enough movies to know the first question a patient asks is 'how long do I have left?' In theory, if the answer to that is far away, or even unknown, that should be good news, but in reality, that kind of uncertainty is hard for anyone to handle. The truth is, of course, life is so often about quality not quantity. If we're the ones getting the news, I think all of us would want to know how long we had left where we're still able to make choices – about what to do, the loved ones we want to spend time with, the way we live. Most of us would also think about what life might look like beyond that stage – will we be aware of our circumstances, will we be in pain, what might our care needs look like or cost, and how will our loved ones cope?

The answers to all of these questions are unique – down to the person involved, their situation and the condition. Advances in modern medicine mean people are living longer and more fully with all kinds of conditions, from rare syndromes to diseases which used to be considered untreatable. But when it comes to long illnesses there are some that sadly remain so common that almost all us will be touched by them, either as patient, carer, friend or relative. Dementia (including its most common form: Alzheimer's), cancer (in many forms) and stroke are diseases we've almost all lost someone too, and most likely over a long period of time.

The early mourning that can happen in this period is known as anticipatory grief. It's a particularly disorienting kind of grief as not only will your feelings be incredibly complex – usually a cocktail of sadness and anxiety, anger and exhaustion – but you'll also probably be asking why you're feeling these things when your loved one is still with you. I've known lots of people struggle with this, and many have felt they can't ask for support – that they're only 'allowed' it after death has happened.

But the agony of this grief can begin way before the actual death, and it's important to feel you can ask for help at any point. Some people feel guilty for thinking about an approaching death, while others ask if they're wishing time away by saying goodbye 'early'. If you are facing saying farewell to someone, it's totally understandable that you will have many goodbyes – a first one to the person they were before illness perhaps, another to the person they become. Other people who've always lived with life-limiting conditions will tell you that all you really need to do is see the person not the condition. We are people, more than a collection of symptoms and treatments.

Of course, if you are beginning your grieving early, it doesn't somehow mean you're 'getting it out of the way early'. Often people feel guilty because at some stage they have wished for death to take their loved one so as not to prolong their pain. None of us can bear to see those we love in pain, miserable or completely reliant on invasive care, especially if we know the person at the heart of it all wouldn't have wanted to live that way.

Knowing that you're in your final days can change a person. I've known so many people find reserves of inner strength, or burly blokes reduced to tears. But often people want to go out of this life in same spirit they've lived it. I've seen people who've always played the joker in life who are still able to crack jokes on their deathbed, or fiercely inde-pendent friends who've refused treatment at the end and said they were ready to go and told their families not to argue.

Others ask for their loved one to fight, when all the one in pain wants to do is sleep and not wake up. The person praying for them to fight is aware that this can be for purely selfish reasons – they can't bear to let go, even though they know it's hard for the other person to stay. I was affected directly by this with both my mother and my sister Bernie, but it was different for me for each of them.

With Mum, by her last days, I was praying for the end, because the here and now was simply horrible for her to bear. But with Bernie, even though I knew it was coming for a long while, I couldn't allow myself to actually accept it. Bernie didn't either, for a long time, but I do remember, a few weeks before she died, she said to us, 'I've fought for a long time, haven't I? I mean, I really have.' I somehow knew at that moment, she was kind of asking our permission to let go, and stop fighting. As painful as it was, I had to let her know it was okay if she'd had enough.

A friend of mine, Anna, recalls the shock of hearing that her 50-year-old mother had been diagnosed with a form of early-onset dementia.

'She'd fallen down some steps one day, and Dad phoned an ambulance because she started to act confused afterwards. They took her to hospital, gave her a scan and that was it, the next day they told us it was dementia. I just couldn't believe it, she was only 50, but the changes in her were dramatic and accelerating. Do you know, she never came out of hospital or nursing homes for almost twelve years before she died.'

'So when did you start to grieve for your mum?' I asked Anna. 'Was it when she got the diagnosis or after she passed away?'

'Neither,' Anna said. 'I'd say it was about a year after her diagnosis. By then, she didn't know who I was any more, and this was especially hard on my kids, who were still quite young then. They couldn't understand why my mum had changed from being a funny, cuddly nanna into this person they didn't recognise and who didn't know them. A person who scowled at them and pushed them away at times. It was just awful. Some days I'd go and Mum was crying and I couldn't help her. She lost the ability to speak and had to be PEG fed. She was quickly completely reliant on the nurses. Dad couldn't have taken her home either. She had so many other complications, he could never have looked after her in the way that was needed.'

Anna said at that point she had to accept the fact that she had already lost her mum, and the grieving was terrible because she was trapped between life and death.

'She was physically there, but it wasn't her,' she said, crying as she remembered, 'and as time passed, it tortured me that I was already acting as if she'd died. We have a big family so, over the years, I'm ashamed to say now, but my visits dwindled down from daily to twice a week, and each visit for twelve years was like a physical pain for me as she became worse and I was powerless to help.'

'And after she finally died, did it hit you all over again?' I asked. 'Or was it like a blessing, really, as you'd already said your goodbyes emotionally?'

Anna thought for a few moments and then said, 'Yes, I'd said goodbye to my mum years earlier, and had grieved that loss for a long time, but the day she died, and especially the funeral day, it was a different kind of grief that hit me. A sobbing, heartbreaking pain and realisation that Mum really had gone. I thought it had been painful when I first accepted losing her years before, but this was another level. Guilt and torturing myself that I hadn't done enough to alleviate her suffering almost suffocated me, and in fact now, four years on, it still sometimes overwhelms me. I might have a dream about Mum, and in my dreams she's always fit and well, and then when I wake, I mourn all over again that she's not here.'

Dementia has so many forms that it's often impossible to put plans in place – everyone's prognosis and changing care needs are different. But it is true that often in the early stages it seems inappropriate to discuss people's wishes for their care and funeral, as they might have sustained periods of seeming completely normal; then, by the time the illness really kicks in, it's often too late to discuss plans and family are left to make all the arrangements themselves, guessing what their loved one would want. This is one of those situations where planning ahead really helps – something all of us can do before any sign of illness.

If you're a carer for someone with dementia, it's important to look after yourself too if you can – even if you feel like you're on duty twenty-four-seven. Whether you're looking after your loved one at home or visiting them in care, it comes down to that old saying: you can't pour from an empty cup. With a long illness, the support you need might take a different form to someone handling a sudden loss. You're in a marathon – running a race you can't stop, and yet don't want to end. You can feel alone even when you're with your loved one if they've gone through personality change or lost the mental sharpness they once had, or if they've lost speech or other communication. There are lots of organisations that can provide specialist help and advice for dementia carers and I'd really recommend getting in touch. I know lots of people don't contact the charities that offer support because they feel it's hopeless – that, because we don't yet have a cure, there's nothing that can be done. But in fact, support for carers and sufferers alike can be transformative even if it's focussed on quality of life rather than curing anything.

But many of the long illnesses mentioned earlier don't alter a person's personality, awareness or memory at all – they're still 'them' even when facing a long road to the end. The best thing you can do supporting someone in this situation is listen to them and take their lead. Do they want to share their deepest worries? Often people are concerned not so much about their own condition but about their families, or knowing when to switch active treatment to palliative care, whether they can stay at home or when they might need round-the-clock care. You won't have answers for many of the questions, but by not being afraid of them you can offer incredible support. Experts suggest that we should ask questions that will give us clues to a dying person's wishes, such as: what do you worry about? How can I help? Is there anything you want to talk about? Don't rebuff anything they say by reacting with platitudes such as 'that's a long way off'. If they are talking about their end of life with you, it's because they trust you to listen to all of their fears. Time can seem to freeze when someone is told they have a terminal illness, but as the weeks and months go on and all treatment options have been tried, then time speeds up again, and it's crucial to not leave things unsaid. The dying person may want to tell loved ones how much they mean to them, they may want to make apologies or amends for past mistakes. If you can help them in this, then it can be a hugely rewarding, if very emotional, role to take on.

Other people might choose to ask their darker questions to professionals and instead want to have everyday conversations with you – gossip and TV programmes, funny stories or just the news headlines. When you're terminally ill, sometimes even the most conscientious patient can get fed up of talking about their condition and just want to feel normal for a while.

For some people, knowing the clock is ticking on their remaining days inspires them to incredible feats. We've all probably watched or read about people like Dame Deborah James, known to millions as Bowel Babe, who raised not just incredible amounts of money, but also huge awareness around the subject of bowel cancer. The same is true of legendary rugby player Rob Burrow, whose fundraising for motor neurone disease means that there will be an institute in his name spearheading research into the condition that saw him die at only 41. Alongside his incredible fundraising, his widow Lindsey shared after his death that he had also recorded messages for his children so they will still have his words with them as they grow up. It's an incredible thing to do, and while it is no doubt a really poignant process to go through, it can bring huge comfort to all involved.

And when the time does finally come to say goodbye, it's worth being prepared for the strength of emotion that comes. You might not have the crippling shock that someone mourning a sudden death might have, but you will likely have a huge sense of emptiness. This is often because your life was put on hold for a long time whilst caring for a loved one.

Losing your identity as a carer is complex – it can take a long time for someone to get used to living for themselves again. Hopefully you will have had time to prepare, but living through loss is always a different experience to anticipating it. There can be great comfort in knowing you helped your loved one, and they have probably even told you that they want you to go and live your life without them, but adjustment isn't easy. The mix of relief and sorrow, anger and apprehension is bound to take time to process. Trust your instincts; some people decide the only way to cope with the loss after such a long illness is by doing something drastic to ring the changes – setting off on a backpacking adventure or embracing a new career. Other people feel small steps is what will point them in the right direction – staying close to the memories. Whichever path you choose, remember that living our lives true to ourselves is one of the best ways you can honour the memory of those we've lost.

The Long Goodbye

I said goodbye some time ago, to the person I once knew,
The love I felt was still the same, the heart was always you.
But the you I knew had gone away, had found some better place,
Leaving only a familiar body, and a heartbreakingly familiar face.

The you that's gone forever now, I cared for, very much,
But I missed the old you, your humour, your kisses and your touch.
I know that somewhere deep inside, some part of you clung on,
Until you could no longer fight, then what made you *you* was gone.

Goodbye for now my loved one, until we meet once more,
And when we do, I'm certain, you'll be you again for sure.

Chapter 15

NO TIME FOR
FAREWELLS

ALL OF US at some time have struggled to find some words of comfort for a grieving friend – and I bet most of us when coping with the shock of hearing of a sudden passing have reached for some saying or familiar phrase to suggest a quick passing is a merciful one. There may indeed be some truth in that – but in the grip of sudden grief, it doesn't feel like that.

Often people reach for phrases like 'at least they didn't suffer' as a kind sentiment, but it's not always much help when you're deep in shock. We looked at the harsh reality of a slow farewell in the chapter before, and I can understand why many of us talk about how we'd rather go 'out like a light' or 'quietly in our sleep' – but I wanted to offer some room here to talk about how an unexpected death leaves those left behind feeling.

We talk about 'natural causes' in situations like this, and we all know that death is part of life, but when it comes out of the blue it doesn't feel very 'natural' – we're too traumatised by the news to think about the causes. So how do you start to mourn, let alone move forward when your life is turned upside down in an instant?

I started this book talking about my sister-in-law Linzie. When she died so suddenly and so young, it seemed completely senseless to me. Even though, medically, her death was a 'natural' death, to me there was nothing natural about the sudden death of a 26-year-old. I think because we were the same age it was even more incomprehensible for me, because it made me question everything. I cried so many tears after losing Linzie, and I grieved for such a long time afterwards.

Because there is no kind of preparation or explanation that seems acceptable for this type of death, our grieving is powerful and prolonged. But sometimes, it can take some time for it to actually begin, because no one can truly mourn when they're in shock. It's not easy, but do expect the stages of grief to come not in waves but almost in pulses as your mind, body and spirit try to understand this brutal shift to your reality. It might feel like a tear or a fracture, you might feel lost as you look for a cause or a reason. Most of all, it probably won't feel real. It's a cliché, but time is the only thing that will help that – and you should be as gentle with yourself as you can, and accept the support of others while your brain tries to come to terms with the news.

It's a tough truth that a lot of sudden deaths bring with them more questions than we can cope with in the eye of the storm. Without an illness or advanced age to warn us and put our body and mind in danger mode, we might feel like this terrible event has caught us vulnerable and unprepared, has taken our loved one like a bolt from the blue. Almost before the emotion hits, you might find yourself wanting to scream out 'what?', 'how?' or 'why?'.

We've all had family, friends or even colleagues who've been felled in an instant by a heart attack or stroke, an aneurysm or embolism. But until the doctors have been able to find the cause, you might feel in limbo. It can feel like you've walked into a TV drama; suddenly there are conversations about post-mortems and inquests – all words we find incredibly hard to say – and it certainly might feel like you've woken up in someone else's life.

This is where the professionals are essential – those who come before the grief counsellors and funeral providers we've discussed already. In these first hours, you need to rely on people whose job it is to help you in the immediate crisis. The medics or even police are there to guide you through the first moments of trauma. There can be so much unexpected process and procedure to get through – the coroner's office, the paperwork, even the language around a sudden death can feel alien and hard to understand. If you can, take a friend or relative to these appointments to help you process and remember the details and information. It's one of those sad truths, but when you've been through it once, you might be the person who can offer support to someone else in the future.

Of course, you might react in the exact opposite way. I know lots of people who've been completely numb after an unexpected loss. We don't all react in the same way – you might be lost for words, or find yourself needing to talk a mile a minute to get the words out of your head. You might need to be alone to process what's happened, or you may find yourself craving normality and wanting to do the supermarket shop just to be around people.

While some people find comfort in the ordinary routines of life, working out what to carry on with and what to reassess isn't easy. I spoke to someone who'd had to cope with the sudden loss of a friend at work. Many of us spend so much of our time with colleagues, it can feel incredibly traumatic when one of our close workmates dies – especially if we need to carry on.

'When my workmate died unexpectedly of an undiagnosed heart condition it was a shocking and difficult time,' the friend told me. 'I arrived at work one sunny summer morning to be told she had died overnight. She was around five years younger than me, fit and healthy, and had always been a really vibrant, fun, hard-working person. We worked together on lots of projects and when she died we were just finishing a big project that we had been working on for months.

'It was difficult in two ways – the first was the shock. She had been absolutely fine when I waved goodbye to her on the Friday before, and then on the Sunday afternoon she started to feel unwell and went to bed and just died.

'The other side which was hard was the practical side – the fact we were workmates. I then had to finish off lots of the project we had been working on together but that she would never see completed. Most people around us knew what had happened but there were a few who were still copying her into emails and we had to explain several times that she had died.

'The project itself was an awful lot of work, and we wanted it to be incredible, knowing how hard she had worked on it. Of course, because we were workmates, someone new had to be hired in her place, which meant the replacement had to take on lots of half-finished work and also knew people would be thinking about our much-loved friend and colleague.

'I carried on working in that job for quite some time after the loss, and sometimes I'd have a smile thinking about what her response would have been to the ups and downs of working life – if we ever had a pointless meeting, I could just hear her saying, "Well, that was a total waste of time, wasn't it?" and laughing. I still miss her and think about her a lot, but with lots of fondness and not as much sadness as I once had.'

Even when you've had the first few hours and days to get answers to the 'what' and 'how' of sudden loss, it's likely you'll find yourself coming back to the 'why'. As humans, we've evolved to look for patterns, for reasons and causes. Sometimes there might be something we can understand – an answer to cling to. But often, as in so many bereavements, there is no easy 'why', and making peace with that is one of the longest parts of your journey through grief. I find myself coming back to that old saying, that grief is love's twin. We mourn because we've loved, and if you've had to go suddenly from love to grief, it can feel like the love has been swapped for grief. It's only as the days pass that we come to realise the love hasn't been replaced by grief, and that under all the emotion, the love remains.

No rhyme or reason

I would never have been ready
To say goodbye to you.
The big plans and the small,
The times that lay ahead,
You were in all that I imagined,
In everything I planned.

So bright a light, so wide a smile,
So big a heart, so quick to help.
I can't see how that ends.
Without sign or warning,
No grand farewell,
Just fierce and blinding shock.

Your last surprise, this final bow,
A trick I cannot solve.
And now I know, what I see was always true.
If I'd had a lifetime more,
I would never have been ready,
To say goodbye to you.

Chapter 16

A TRAGIC DEATH

LOSING SOMEONE SUDDENLY is a shock as well as a sorrow, as we explored in the last chapter. We are left feeling at sea, rocked by feelings we were completely unprepared for. But the coping strategies that may help us cope with a sudden death due to physical illness are not always the ones that will help in one of the hardest roads to travel: experiencing loss by tragedy. Of course, tragedy is a tricky word – we feel the tragic nature of any close loss, but what it might be helpful to touch on here are those cruel losses that happen abruptly by accident or violence, or the complex factors around mental health crisis and suicide.

The grief triggered in these circumstances can be so wholly unexpected that it can lead us to feel almost totally unconnected from our old life. Yolanda Clarke from Cruse Bereavement Support, and Tracey from Co-op Funeralcare explained that these feelings are completely normal, and in such tragic cases grief can reach far beyond those who knew that person.

We often talk about feeling on your own after the death of a close connection – but the flip side is just as hard to handle. How do you cope when your loss is public – if you're struggling to process the news at the same time as it's in the papers? I know from experience that handling the press can be complicated, so my advice here is simple: put yourself first. The rest of the world can wait – do what feels right for you.

But just because other people know what's happened it doesn't automatically mean you'll have support. 'A sudden or shocking death,' Tracey said, 'can affect the whole community, particularly if the cause of death was suicide. This is because it's not only the family that feel a sense of guilt that they didn't see it coming, that they didn't spot any signs – friends, colleagues and acquaintances may also believe this.'

'And that's why the reactions can also be so different under these circumstances,' Yolanda went on. 'People will cross the street, or start an imaginary phone call, just to avoid speaking to you, because they feel so guilty and genuinely don't know what they can possibly say to comfort you.'

UK Mental Health Ambassador and former *Love Island* contestant Dr Alex George lost his younger brother to suicide in 2020. He joined me on one of my *Let's Start Talking* podcasts to speak about how it affected him.

'It was just a normal day,' he explained, 'a lovely day in fact, because I was out having lunch with a few friends after the pandemic and the UK's lockdown had just been eased. It was so nice to be out and about and seeing friends again. During that lunch was when I got the call from my dad to tell me my brother had died. I was completely thrown.'

'Did you know it was suicide?' I asked.

'No, not initially, but then a couple of hours later I got a second call from Dad to tell me that he'd taken his own life. It was like he'd died twice that day, just awful.'

'Was it something you saw coming?' I asked. 'Was he suffering with his mental health at the time?'

'Well, he had been struggling with the whole lockdown experience,' Alex said, 'so yes, I suppose his mental health wasn't in the best condition, but what made it even worse for me was that I'd actually been working in that field. In fact just two weeks before his death I had produced a video giving advice to people on how to look after your mental health during lockdown, so I felt so guilty that I'd not been able to help my own brother.'

'But you weren't to know,' I said, 'and they say that suicide is a chosen decision, so I don't think anybody could have really helped.'

'You're right,' Alex said, 'but it doesn't make it feel any better. My brother was only 19, with his whole life ahead of him. He was going to med school, set to become a doctor, and then suddenly all of that was gone. You know, I'm considered to be some kind of expert in mental health, and yes, I found that my training helped me to help my parents and family, but I couldn't help myself, I was just a mess. In the end I had to reach out to professionals, to my friends and family, to anyone I could. I had to accept my own limitations and get the help I needed.'

Dr Alex also told me a few surprising facts that I had no idea about. In the UK, the number one cause of death at age 35 is suicide, for men and women. And during the first year after giving birth to a child, a woman is more likely to die from suicide than any other cause. It's tragic, it really is. As hard as it can be to find the words, breaking the taboo is one of the best ways we can help.

'Because no one likes to talk about suicide,' Alex went on, 'I'm trying to make it more acceptable to speak about it. People often say "committed" suicide, which makes it feel almost criminal. These days we prefer to say "died by suicide" rather than "committed".'

The sudden shock of a tragic accident can also shape the way we grieve. A 30-year-old friend of mine, Hayley, lost her fiancé, George, aged just 24, two years ago.

'He simply kissed me goodbye that morning, just like every other morning, ruffled my baby son's curls and then set off to work. That was the last time I ever saw him alive.'

George was a mechanic who worked at a friend's garage in the next town. He drove to work every weekday and set off very early in the morning. The week before he died he had saved up enough money to buy Hayley a beautiful diamond engagement ring and had proposed over a romantic dinner at a local restaurant. It had been raining heavily throughout the night and was still pouring down when he set off that final morning.

'The police turned up at my door and told me that paramedics had said that his car had aquaplaned on a bad bend. Witnesses said that he'd been driving safely, but had no chance on that bend. The car had flipped and killed my George instantly. I was completely and utterly devastated.'

Hayley was in tears as she relived that day, and I could feel her pain was still so raw.

'I felt like I'd lost everything in that moment,' she said. 'My beautiful future that I'd seen so clearly, a loving stepfather to my little boy who George doted on, and my best friend. All at once, all gone.'

'And now?' I asked. 'Is it easier two years down the line?'

'It actually is,' Hayley admitted. 'I will never forget George. I have his pictures up everywhere and I talk about him all the time, but despite me believing that I couldn't possibly live without him, I am doing. At first it was for my son. I had to create some normality for his sake, but as time went on I realised that actually, I was living. I was laughing at times and enjoying the simple things and enjoying time with friends again, so yes, it gets easier.'

'But do you still have your bad days when it all becomes too much?' I asked.

'I do, and when that happens I try to keep myself busy if I've got my son with me, and if it's too much I ask my mum to take him for a few hours so that I can wallow a bit in my memories. Those social media memories that pop up can really catch you by surprise, and they can be a killer to deal with, but now I find I'm able to have that bit of sad reflection but not stay in it, if you know what I mean. Like, I can then find a memory that's funny and I can giggle about it. It's weird but definitely not as painful any more.'

So, no matter how painful the circumstances, it seems we can find a way to move forward with life. We really are resilient creatures when you think about it, and we somehow manage to claw our way back from the most horrific pain and heartache. The recurring theme seems to be that after we lose a dearly loved one, we truly believe at the time that we can't possibly go on, and yet we do. They say time is a great healer, and I never really believed that, but what I do believe is that as time passes, we change, and we learn to live a different life, a life where our past and our future intertwine comfortably and we are able to live with both.

Losing someone suddenly in any way that feels tragic, accidental or even criminal is particularly hard for us to accept. These deaths are truly hard to bear as they seem so far away from reality. We read about them, hear of them on the news, but we never imagine it could happen to us, and when it does, it seems almost unreal. We don't believe it, we can't believe it. It completely floors us, emotionally and physically. We feel actual pain as we struggle to breathe and make sense of what we're being told.

When it comes to deaths by violence, people talk of their sense of loss being physical – a gut reaction to the deep injustice. And while the legal justice system is there to try to bring some kind of balance or reparation, it's not there to address the emotional fallout. It can be some relief if someone is convicted but it can't solve the pain, and I'm in awe of the strength of many victims' families who come through such tough circumstances and build something positive out of their pain – families and friends who build campaigns, change laws or fund charities all in honour of their loved one.

This is what gives me hope – even from the darkest times, we see people doing amazing things in honour of their lost loved one. If we can be even a small part of helping someone in that situation, we can show what community can achieve, and find faith in the strength of people to come together.

The Depth

They say grief is silence,
But I never knew how deep.
They say grief is a wound,
But I never knew how deep.
They say grief is a rage,
But I never knew how deep.
They say grief is confusion,
But I never knew how deep.
They say grief is a darkness,
But I never knew how deep.
But deeper still beneath the silence,
The hurt, the anger and the loss,
Through the dark that stops my eyes,
Is something deeper still.
They say that grief is love,
But I never knew how deep.

Chapter 17

A GRIEVING CHILD

I KNEW I wanted to devote a whole chapter to this subject as I feel it's really important to recognise that children grieve very differently to adults. They haven't yet built up enough life experiences to know what to do with such huge, over-whelming feelings, and it can be hard for us to watch them grapple with such big feelings and not know how best to help them, especially if we're grieving with them. It can also go the other way – that children are too young to filter their feelings and can make everyone around them feel better as we're struck by their honesty; and let's admit it, their humour and curiosity can be a tonic too. We touch on it briefly in the chapter about losing a pet, and that's hard enough for a child – usually their first ever experience of death – but it's a completely different matter when a person who was close to them passes away.

While there may be many commonalities in all our experi-ences of grief and loss, every person, family, community and culture is unique, as we've seen. So it's unsurprising that the understanding and expression of that grief varies too. In your family it might be that you cry openly, whilst other families might find this completely inappropriate.

When we experience a loss, we as adults might feel that we should try to protect our children by not telling them what's happened. This is perfectly understandable – we all want to shield our kids from pain – but it is ultimately much more helpful and supportive to tell them the truth in a language they can understand. This reduces confusion and gives them the opportunity to adjust to the loss, rather than leaving them to try figure out for themselves what happened. Even babies and very young children recognise when someone is no longer in their lives, especially if that person was around a lot.

We need to be as honest and clear as possible when explaining things to them. There are lots of charities that can support you with age-appropriate language, and almost all of them will say that euphemisms and metaphors – while often beautiful – are not always helpful for children. Gone to sleep, gone away, passed over – they are more likely to make a child imagine all sorts of situations rather than coming to terms with the fact that a person they knew has died and they won't see them again.

This will naturally depend on what kind of loss has occurred – a sudden loss will need a different treatment to an anticipated one, a tragic death will need different conversations to passing away from natural causes at the end of a long life. But being clear is always helpful – and you can of course be factual while gentle.

It's often not enough to simply say, for example, 'Grandma has died.' They will want to know why or how. If it was old age or illness then it's worth being as clear as possible. If we can name the illness, it can help children feel like it's not something that's going to instantly happen to them or other people they know and love. 'Grandma has died from a disease called cancer,' can sound more formal than how we might imagine speaking to a child, and you'd naturally lead up to it gently – but it's valuable to include plain facts like this in the conversation. If we just say, 'Grandma was ill and then she died', then whenever they hear of someone being ill, however minor, they might assume now that they too will die.

We also need to make it clear to a child that, in most circumstances, the death was nobody's fault and certainly that there's nothing they could have done to change things.

When speaking to a child about death, make sure to ask them if they have any worries or questions. I'm sure they will have lots, and they can come out at strange times. Experts have told me that the most common two are:

- Will you die? Will I die? When will you or I die?
- Is the person coming back? Will I see them again?

The response to the first one must be honest. 'We all die at some point, when our bodies stop working, but hopefully we live for many, many years, and we can always play and be together until we are both very, very old.' To the second question we should reiterate what we've already told them. 'No, sweetie, Grandma died, remember? That means we can't see her again, but we can talk about her lots, and look at all her beautiful photographs.'

What you tell a child about what happens after we die will depend on your own beliefs and what you'd like your child to believe. But it's worth remembering that they might repeat this to other friends or people in their lives, so make sure other important people in the child's life know what's happened. Teachers always like to know so they can support the child and be ready to answer any questions appropriately or understand any emotional aftershocks the child might have.

It is thought that a baby or toddler, even though they can't communicate it, also feels the effects of losing a loved one and reacts to it. They will often show increased separation anxiety, and seek extra attention. They might start to regress and take longer to reach expected milestones. They don't understand the concept of permanence so if they can talk they may seek out or ask for the person who died and have an increased need for nurturing. All this is normal, and to help them through it we need to provide them with the comfort they need, so lots of cuddles, rocking and soft speaking or singing to soothe them, and most importantly, a good routine. Settled times for eating, sleeping and waking up provide even the youngest children with the stability they need in order to feel safe and secure.

For an older child or a teenager, grief can be even more difficult to cope with than for a younger child. Already they are experiencing hormonal changes within themselves and if a close family member dies during this time it can really mess with their heads. As adults, if we tell someone that a loved one has died, we can rely on the response we would receive. We would get instant empathy and support. A teenager on the other hand has a very different set of peers and they might be met with an awkward silence at best, or responses like, 'you're kidding!' or 'no way! What did they die from?' Both unhelpful responses and are often the reason that a teenager will decide it's better to suffer in silence and not speak about it with their peers.

Teenagers feel negative emotions far more acutely than we adults do, so often they might feel shame, guilt or remorse and remember how they weren't as close as they should have been, or they might have said hurtful things that they definitely didn't mean, and all of this plays havoc with their lives. They might find they can't sleep as readily as they could before or that they can't concentrate at school. They might go off their food and stop doing the activities they used to enjoy, and they will, more often than not, take their feelings out on those closest to them. This in turn makes them feel worse and the cycle never seems to end.

It's difficult for us as adults to know how to help a grieving teen, because for most of the time they seem to push us away, but we can help. We can do this by allowing them space when they need it, by encouraging them to talk when they're in the mood, and if not to us then to a friend or teacher who they trust. Offer hugs and don't get upset if they decline it: the last thing they need is to feel they are upsetting you. Some teens may feel the need to be a pillar of strength, so letting them show and work through their feelings can empower them. Talk about the person who died and share funny memories if you can, and also let your teen know that you are grieving yourself so you absolutely understand how difficult it is.

It might be helpful to create a family tree at this point, because it might surprise you but some teens aren't always aware of all the various family connections. We assume they know, but far too often they don't. A family tree helps them to put all the pieces together and it can be a time for sharing special childhood memories of your own. This all serves to help a teenager feel more connected to the wider family, and can help with the grieving process as it anchors them to know exactly where they fit and who surrounds them. You could buy them a special gift like a bracelet or a pendant in memory of their lost loved one, something they can keep and refer to if and when they like.

The most important thing we can do, however, is to acknowledge that children grieve too, often more intensely than we do, and, no matter what we are going through ourselves, we must be honest and open, and make them a part of the grieving and healing process.

I've also seen some incredible initiatives recently where nurseries and care homes combine – toddlers and the elderly can form incredible relationships – and often both groups have a more practical relationship with loss than us adults in the midst of life. They can provide incredible support, joy and understanding – even at opposite ends of life.

Do also have faith in the resilience and generosity of children. You will be able to make a judgement call on whether they are at an age where attending the funeral will be important for them, and you'll often find that, where children have to go through the incredibly tough experience of losing a peer, then they can form really powerful support networks among themselves. I also know so many people who when their own grief threatened to overwhelm them told me, 'If it wasn't for the kids, I don't know how I'd carry on' – and it's true that the younger generations do not just give us hope, but their dependence on us can keep us going. Often the usual demands of raising a family – cooking, cleaning, school runs and so on, may get bumpy during grief, but it's always worth letting a child know that their presence and needs are not a burden, even during the worst of times, and instead that their role in your life is often what gives you the strength to move forward.

Through the eyes of a child

Why is this happening? This is all wrong,
First you were here, and now you are gone.
No one is speaking, just so many tears,
What about me, my worries and fears?

I go to my room where I cry on my own,
I've really never felt so truly alone.
My anger builds up with nowhere to go,
I want to scream out, "I'm here, you know!'

I know that you loved me, did you know that too?
I feel like I might not have often said that to you.
Right now I need comfort, and for someone to see,
I can't cope with these feelings inside of me.

I'll wait for a break in the sadness downstairs,
Before joining them, if anyone cares.
Please someone see me, and what I'm going through,
I know you're all hurting, but I'm hurting too.

Chapter 18

THE UNSAID

WE THINK OF a death as an ending – but life is messy, and death is often an interruption, leaving things unfinished, words unspoken. When you're coping with the loss of a loved one, feelings are often complicated, even beyond the sorrow and the anger we've already discussed. So, what happens if things get more complicated still and you discover after someone's death that there were things you never knew about them?

I think we've all read the stories about people having undiscovered second families turn up at funerals, or wills being read and a secret child being named. Sometimes the secrets you discover might not be as dramatic as a whole other life, but often I hear of friends who, when faced with the difficult task of packing up a loved one's possessions, have come across a letter or memento that shows even those closest to us might have not told us everything. Sometimes these discoveries can raise a smile, and at other times they can leave us wounded by things left unspoken.

For so much of this book we've concentrated on the pain of losing a loved one, but I wanted to take a moment to explore the question of bidding farewell to people you have a difficult relationship with. Perhaps you've lost someone you'd fallen out with, or perhaps it's someone who's done you great harm – either way, their passing can cause emotional ripples that can leave you floundering, and without a way to understand how you feel.

I remember speaking to a friend who'd recently been to her aunt's funeral.

'She was 64 when she died,' my friend said, 'and obviously I'd known her all my life, she was my aunty! However, after the service – it was a full Catholic burial and mass – we all went to my aunt's favourite working men's club and somebody cranked up the music and the karaoke machine, just as she'd have wanted. But I noticed that lots of people seemed to be whispering and had strange expressions on their faces. I know funerals are emotional times but I felt there was something more than the usual sorrow and smiles. I decided to ask my cousin what was going on. She was pretty shocked but shared with me what she'd discovered. Apparently, the elderly man dressed in a smart suit who had been standing at the back of the church on his own had flown over from Spain to pay his respects. Of course, there are often lots of people you don't know at a funeral, but this one took the biscuit. It turned out Aunty Sylvia, who'd been jetting off to

Benidorm by herself for over thirty years because her husband wouldn't fly, had been having a secret holiday romance with that guy for two weeks every bloody year for thirty years!'

'Oh my Lord!' I said, 'what a shock. Your uncle must have been mortified.'

'Well actually, he passed away last year,' she went on, 'so hopefully he never knew, but my cousins, they were gobsmacked! I shouldn't admit this, but honestly, they were shocked, sure, but there was a grin on their faces. I think they were half impressed that she'd been able to do this for all that time and yet still be a devoted wife and mother when she got back from her holidays. Puts a whole new spin on going off on your jollies, doesn't it?'

It certainly does, and I have to admit I still can't help smiling when I remember that story. It turns out life is never quite done with surprises.

But surprises can be hard too. The next story I have to share may feel traumatic for some, and I have had to change names in order to share it with you. But death doesn't always wipe the slate clean, and bad deeds aren't absolved by passing away. This personal story involves a particularly devastating type of abuse and it's something that naturally most of us find hard to read about, but I know it's important that victims are given a place to speak up. This came from a young woman who got in touch via a friend when she knew I was writing this book. I shall call her Rebecca.

'From being a little girl, my dad would come into my bedroom at night, before I even knew the word "abuse",' Rebecca said. 'I'm a twin, and if I cried or made a noise, Dad would threaten me, say that he'd hurt my sister instead if I couldn't keep quiet. That was enough to shut me up. My sister was smaller than me and always poorly, and I loved her so much, I'd have done anything to protect her.'

'Just to get this right,' I asked, 'are we talking sexual abuse? I'm sorry if I'm wrong – I want to be clear, and I know physical, sexual or emotional abuse can all bring their own trauma.'

Rebecca nodded. 'You're probably wondering what this has to do with your book, and with grief, but I think it has a lot to do with it,' she said. 'You see, this went on from me being 6 years old until I was 14. Mum was a bingo fanatic, she'd go any chance she got, and Dad was very clever at getting her out of the house and offering to be "Mr Mum" for the evening, at least twice a week.'

'Did you ever think about telling your mum as you got older? Or talking to a teacher or other adult?' I asked.

Rebecca smiled. 'Every single person I've ever told has asked that exact question,' she said, 'and that's where it starts to get complicated. You're going to be horrified at my explanation, but despite what he was doing to me, despite my eventually knowing how wrong it was, I loved him! Apart from those terrible nights, he was a great dad. He took us to theme parks, to the cinema, he always made sure we had nice clothes and good food, he worked hard and gave Mum everything she needed. It was just what happened at night. I hated it, but had no words to describe it, no way of understanding it even, so somehow I learned to tune it out of my mind and separated it from the rest of me, my life and our family life.'

'How awful,' I said, 'but surely you can't blame yourself; you were just a child. Even at 14, when it stopped, you were still a child. Why did it stop then, what changed?'

'He died,' Rebecca said, flatly. 'He had a massive heart attack while he was in bed with Mum one night and was pronounced dead when the paramedics arrived.'

I was shocked as I listened, and allowed Rebecca to carry on in her own time.

'And that's where it got even more complicated,' she went on. 'You see, even though he'd hurt me for all those years, physically and emotionally, the grief I experienced after losing him almost crushed me. It was just enormous.'

Complicated was the right word. I was stunned as I listened to Rebecca explain that she never told either her mum or her sister about the abuse, even after her dad's death.

'They were grieving the man they knew, not the man I knew, and I couldn't add to that,' she said. 'I was 34 when I eventually told them. I'd had counselling since I was 20, because I was lost, completely lost. I hated myself for grieving a man who had done all that stuff to me, and I thought it must say something about myself, like I was some kind of weirdo. I mean, I should have rejoiced at his passing, right?'

I didn't know how to answer if I'm being honest. How could I possibly understand that, how can anyone who's not been in that awful situation? But I wanted to know more.

'So, when you finally got through your counselling and told your mum and sister, was that the start of your healing?'

'Well,' she said, 'as I'm sure you can imagine, Mum and Emma were devastated. But at the same time, I think they wanted to not believe me. They'd ask things like, "are you absolutely sure? You weren't having nightmares or something? But you were Dad's favourite!" It sort of brought it all crashing down on me again and I felt myself being taken back to those days. However, my therapist had told me to simply tell them my story, allow them some time to take it in, tell them I needed their support and then to leave it in their hands.'

'So, you did that?' I asked. 'And did they ever understand?'

'Well, we're okay now, if that's what you mean,' Rebecca said, 'but I'm not sure they'll ever understand. They don't get how I could have cried so much for him, and they don't get why I've had to forgive him to move on. They believe me now, of course, but they won't ever mention his name in front of me. In fact Mum has taken all his photos down. They just don't want to think about it and that's fine by me.

I'm just glad I can finally put it behind me and realise that my grief, no matter how displaced it was, was normal and okay for me, and as an adult now I can see it for what it was. If I hadn't mourned him, I think I'd have been eaten up by anger that I'd never had the chance to get closure, to confront him or report him while he was alive. Forgiveness has been my way of freeing myself, of not letting him control my life even after he's gone. I also stopped waiting for my feelings to be black and white. Abuse leaves you with scars, confusion and a world of things to work through. My grief is a part of that process. Complicated beyond comprehension, but there nevertheless.'

It can't have been easy for Rebecca to share her story, but I believe we shouldn't avoid talking about the dark times because, after all, they are human behaviours, and we shouldn't be afraid to explore even the darkest of subjects. Bringing things into the light is a way of facing our fears, helping heal old wounds and sharing our experiences.

Of course, there are sometimes much happier discoveries to be shared after someone dies, and I've been lucky enough to have heard some of these stories too.

Katie was a middle sibling, and on her mum's side of the family there was only an elderly uncle.

'My younger brother and my older sister were dark-haired and looked just like Mum, whereas I was fair-haired and blue-eyed just like my dad,' Katie told me. 'Every other weekend I'd moan like crazy when Mum would traipse us on two buses to go see her brother because there were no other relatives. I really didn't like him at all; he was grumpy and he was always telling me off. I felt like he favoured the other kids because they looked like his family and I didn't. Daft, I know, but it was always me that bore the brunt of his bad moods.'

I laughed and told her maybe she was just the naughtiest one.

'Maybe,' she smiled, 'but anyway, despite his prolonged ill health, and Mum always saying things like, "oh come on, he might not be here this time next year, we have to go", he lived until he was 84, by which time I was 40. And in the end? He left me his blooming house! Me! I couldn't believe it and neither could my siblings.' She laughed as she said that. 'Mum actually said that he'd always had a soft spot for me, can you imagine? I thought he hated me. Anyway, of course I intend to share my unexpected windfall with my brother and sister. In fact we are all doing the house up just now to put it up for sale, but yes, a really surprising bit of news for me.'

There are lots of surprising stories like this that emerge from the sorrow of grief but one other I should mention came from a widower in his eighties. He had been married to his wife, Anne, for over sixty years, until she died just a year ago.

'The grandchildren offered to come over and help me go through Anne's things,' he told me. 'I hadn't been able to do it myself and they knew I was struggling. Anyway, they got rid of all the bits and bobs that wouldn't have been any good to anyone else, and they were halfway through clearing out the wardrobe, sorting things that would be suitable for the local charity shop, when they came across an old hat box way up on the shelf above the hanging rails. I remember thinking, well there can't be anything important in that because Anne was less than five feet tall, she'd never be able to reach up there without standing on something.'

'What was in it?' I asked, knowing all of us have probably had the tough task of helping clear a relative's home at some point, and know a little of what it's like to find treasures and memories in the middle of the chaos and clutter often left behind at the end of a full life.

'I couldn't believe it and neither could the kids, but there was almost ten thousand pounds in the box! Some of it was old money, even. She'd been saving for years and I never knew. There was a letter too. God knows when she'd written it, but it said something along the lines of: whoever finds this, it's for my funeral and for John. He never could save anything so I've done it for him. Make sure he looks after himself and tell him he's allowed a few drinks out of this, but that's his lot!'

I laughed. 'What a lovely surprise,' I said, 'but I imagine the funeral had already happened?'

'It had,' John said. 'Anne mustn't have realised I'd been paying life insurance for years. She never had to worry about paying for bills or anything, and she never asked. But yes, it had all been sorted and I had money left over so, after going to the bank and depositing it into my account, I went straight to the travel agent with my two granddaughters and told them to book a holiday. They tried to fight me of course and wanted me to have some fun with it, but I insisted. It seemed a lovely way for them to remember their nan.'

I think when we discover something new about a loved one after they die, good or bad, it is almost always cause to reflect that we never know anybody completely, not really. And perhaps it gives us cause to think what people might be surprised to learn about us after we're gone. We all leave a mark on the world and the people who love us – but sometimes, it's not for us to know what our legacy really is.

Complications

Our relationship was difficult, and I often wonder why
That now you're gone I'm hurting and still break down and cry.
Is it for what we could have been? For all the should have beens?
Or is it because I'm free now, is that what all this means?

I know I mourn the loss of who I hoped you'd be,
And I wonder why that never was, if it was down to me.
I hope that you will rest in peace, no matter all that's past,
And know that I forgive you, so I find peace at last.

Chapter 19

NEVER FORGOTTEN

IN THE SHARP sting of immediate grief, it can seem baffling when someone says that no one ever truly dies while they're still remembered, but as our sorrow settles and changes shape, many of us start to feel the truth in that. When you've loved and lost, the impact of that person stays with you always – you are different for having known them and it's the gift we all leave.

But choosing how you remember someone can be an important part of our grief journeys. There's no need to have a formal service, place or object to remember someone by – they're always in our thoughts, after all – but often there is a deep-seated urge to have a focus for our memories and another way of paying tribute to who we've lost.

The most common way we do this is with a headstone in a cemetery or interring ashes in a garden of remembrance. We often associate graveyards with the impossibly sad moment of burial – but they can also be a place of comfort, that you can return to in future years. I find it amazing sometimes to read the carved lines on gravestones or statues from decades or even centuries gone by and realise we all go through the same pain and loss. But I know that cemeteries are just too sad for some people to visit, and can see why great solace can come from having another place to go to. I was talking to someone the other day who'd had a tree planted for a loved one with a national charity, and now feels they can visit that wood and wander through the trees feeling close to them. When I took part in the TV series *The Nolans Go Cruising*, with my sisters, we spent some time at a stately home – close to where the naked man chalk etching, the Cerne Abbas Giant, can be seen in the hills overlooking Dorset. The lovely staff there actually planted a tree in honour of Bernie, to commemorate her life. It was a lovely gesture, and one we've never forgotten.

For some people a place to visit can still feel like a distance they can't bridge between them and their loved one. It turns out that's why many people choose cremation – partly because the thought of scattering ashes somewhere meaningful brings some families a little solace in their grief, while for others it's the opportunity to keep a loved one's ashes nearby. A friend who recently went through a bereavement actually told me about going to collect her grandmother's ashes sometime after the funeral.

'I thought there might be some kind of ceremony or process, but I actually just needed to show some ID and sign a form and there it was – I was given a small urn full of ashes in a velvet bag.'

'How was that?' I asked. 'It must have felt strange.'

'I know a lot of people find the thought unsettling,' my friend continued. 'But I think it actually helped me come to terms with what had happened. It felt like another milestone in my journey, just like when I'd said goodbye to her in the hospital, then at the funeral and now I hugged the urn.'

Another of my friends takes her sister's ashes on every trip with her. 'We always used to holiday together before she got ill,' she said, 'and I promised her that I'd always take her with me. She's been all over the world with me and I always tell myself that I will scatter her ashes somewhere beautiful, but I can't bring myself to do it. Just when I think I will, I think, oh but next year I'm off to such and such, and back she goes in my suitcase.'

For me, I find it comforting that every cat and dog I ever lost is remembered daily. I keep their ashes in little urns in the house and I can always smile as I look at them.

If you find it too hard to make your memory place the same as the grave or site of ashes scattering, there are lots of other ways you can still remember a lost friend, partner or relative. These types of commemoration split into two categories in my mind – public and private. You'll know which, if any, feels right for you. Private ways of remembering the dead can be as simple as a piece of jewellery you wear to feel like you're always carrying them with you in spirit. Other people choose to plant a rose in their garden, make a donation in their name to a charity or perhaps have a memory bear or cushion made. These have become more popular recently and lots of talented sewers and crafters can make beautiful objects out of articles of clothes that remind you of the person you've lost – perhaps a favourite shirt made into a cushion you can hug.

There are many other touching ways you can choose to keep your memories close. One friend of mine has had her mum's handwriting engraved onto a pendant, while another has had the incredible experience of having some precious old photos restored. Unlike our digital pictures today, some of the photographs we all treasure the most are often creased, faded or battered from having moved house, been hung on walls or slipped inside books for years. But restorers can not only help mend rips or folds, they can also recolour and make an image look like it was taken yesterday.

Sometimes, though, despite grieving feeling like a lonely process at times, we need to share our sentiments with the world. I don't know about you, but I always stop and read the little plaques I see on memorial benches. Sometimes funny, sometimes sad, but always personal and surprising, it's a lovely way of sharing someone's favourite spot with others.

There are lots of other ways you can celebrate someone's passions or hobbies after they've gone too – I've seen people sponsor a seat in a football stadium for sports-mad family, or remember how much a friend loved the glamour of showtime by sponsoring a theatre seat in their name.

The joy of picking a way to commemorate someone is you can make it really personal. I know of one village school near me that was gifted a beautiful silver cup that's become their sports day prize, all in memory of a little boy who first found his love of running in those early sack races and egg and spoon dashes!

Of course, if someone's in the fortunate position of leaving some money behind, then a bequest can be a generous way of making a difference to the causes they supported in life. Many people who've known the companionship and joy of owning a pet choose to leave a small gift to animal sanctuaries, while I know of friends who love their seaside holidays who've already chosen to write in a small gift to the lifeboat station near their favourite destination.

As with so many other parts of grief, the key here is doing what feels right to you. I know some people can't even bear to see a single photo of the person they've lost, for fear of it triggering fresh waves of grief, while other people find comfort in hanging almost an art gallery full of snaps. You'll know what brings you comfort – and don't worry if that changes over time. Different things will feel right in different seasons of your life.

You may also remember someone differently if there are younger generations to think about. When children want to know more about relatives they never met, it can be a wonderful thing to share your memories, perhaps leaf through a photo album together – but if I could give you one tip here, it's to take the time to scribble down who people are. We think there will be always be someone who'll be able to remember who that second cousin in a wedding photo was, or which of our great uncles is which – but it's easy to lose track of generations gone by.

I know lots of people who've found their grief has actually motivated them to go and find out more about their own family tree – and sometimes it can be a wonderful thing to realise that we're never truly alone, and there's always branches of a tree somewhere, even if they're far away or we've never met them. Of course there can be surprises too, so do go into it with an open mind.

You'll know when you feel ready to find memories a comfort rather than a sorrow – and while there will always be a bittersweet side to reminiscing, I find it does make that bond you felt in life continue on. I'm lucky to come from a big family, and even though they're not all still here, when I think about those I've lost, I can smile now and see that saying was perhaps right after all – no one is really gone while we can still say their name and think of what a special place they have in our thoughts still.

In Memory Of Me

Don't sit vigil at my grave, for I'm not truly there,
That headstone and those flowers, they show me that you care.
But please don't spend too many hours mourning at that place,
Just think of me and I'm with you, remember my embrace.
In seeds you plant, a bench you choose or maybe kind deeds done,
That is how I'm with you still and how my heart lives on.
Put me in a picture frame, remember things I'd say,
Please have happy memories, I'm with you every day.
If you can say my name, I haven't really gone,
I live within your heart for now, right where I belong.

Chapter 20

A SECOND LOVE

IF THE LANGUAGE we use to talk about death often minimises the loss to try to avoid upsetting people – 'passed away', 'departed', 'a final sleep' – then perhaps the language we use around love is the opposite. When we write about love, in books or films or songs, it's always 'happily ever after', 'my one and only', and 'I'll never fall in love again'. It's a noble feeling but one that doesn't address the fact that more often than not, however happy, blessed or cherished a relationship we've had, one of us will be the leaver, one of us the left behind. In the enormity of grief, if you're the one left behind, it's hard to believe you'll ever feel like yourself again – let alone think about forming a new relationship. But if that day does come, it's worth exploring some of the conflicting emotions that come with it.

After losing a beloved partner, whether you've been together for a short while or married for decades, there may come a time when someone else enters the picture. It might be something you go looking for, or a relationship that blooms when you least expect. Trying to be open-minded is

so often the key. If it is something you decide to seek –
thinking about dating, moving in with someone new or even
remarrying – it can seem scary, unknown or even disloyal.

The decision to think about new relationships is not one
that anyone comes to easily. If this is where you find yourself, don't feel bad if you previously told others – and
yourself – that there would be no next love for you, and
that you had resigned yourself to remaining single for the
rest of your life. If you do then meet someone again and fall
in love, it can be a huge surprise. So many people are
persuaded into trying dating after loss and are convinced it
won't happen for them, and do it more to keep their friends
or family happy – and then are amazed when they do find
there's someone out there for them. Those finding second-
chance love often discover that families and friends are
supportive, yet they give themselves the hardest time.

My friend Rachel had been married to Harry for fifteen
years. It had been a second marriage for both of them and
both were divorced, not widowed. They were such a
fun-loving couple and made the most out of every day.
However, Harry developed a serious lung condition and
was told he only had a maximum of a year left to live. He
was older than Rachel by fifteen years and in his last months
he begged her to live her life fully after he was gone.

'He told me I'd been his carer for long enough, and that
I had to promise him I'd start to live my life again and to
meet someone else that would make me happy,' Rachel

told me. 'I wouldn't promise him any of that, of course, and I told him that no man would ever make me as happy as he had.'

Harry lasted just six months after that conversation before he died, leaving Rachel devastated and alone. She went through severe depression and couldn't look after herself at all in the depths of grief.

'I just felt useless,' she said. 'I turned to drink, didn't clean my house, didn't see the point in dressing nicely any more, or I'd go days wearing the same clothes and not showering. To be truthful, I wanted to die and I would stare at the bottles of Harry's medication and will myself to be brave enough to take it.'

She didn't, and in fact she rang Samaritans and poured her heart out. Through talking to them, she felt strong enough to reach out to a friend who she hadn't connected with since before Harry had been ill.

'She was surprised to hear from me, but when she knew what had happened and how I was feeling, she borrowed her husband's car and came straight round to see me.'

That friend ended up with Rachel in the early hours, helping her to formulate a plan which involved giving her a job in her cleaning company and offering to pick her up and drop her off each day, just to break the cycle of grief. It worked, and soon Rachel started to get back to the person she was, and that was when, out of the blue, she met Norman. He started out as a client and because he was a widower himself, they had lots to talk about. As the months went on, they became closer and Rachel, despite all her reluctance, fell in love all over again.

'It wasn't like a bolt from the blue, not the yearning love that you feel when you're younger,' Rachel explained, 'but kind of a companionship that became deeper as time went on, and I realised one day that I wanted to be with him, permanently. I know he felt the same because he'd said as much, many times, but I used to laugh it off, apart from the time I didn't. I just knew, and although I know it's what Harry wanted for me, I still get pangs of guilt, and I pray that he's happy for me, every day.'

I'm happy for Rachel, that she's found love again, and I know she genuinely loves Norman. I also think it's really important to realise that different isn't wrong when it comes to new love. Not only will a new partner mean a different kind of relationship, but we ourselves change throughout our lives. We feel things differently, react differently, so naturally, we will love differently too. I guess that love is a bit like grief in that respect – it comes in all sorts of shapes and sizes.

It can also be tough for the new partner of the bereaved – as well as being sensitive to someone who's been through a major loss, they might also feel a sense of comparison. A previous partner is often still there in memories – places visited, events recalled, films seen together. That's natural, and learning to embrace a new relationship should never mean shutting off the past or not mentioning a lost loved one's name. But it's worth being aware that there can be tensions too. Sometimes a second partner can believe they need to compete with a ghost, which can cause friction. It can be even more complicated when there are children involved. I'd suggest making sure everyone feels they can discuss their feelings, that no topic is out of bounds – but, of course, remembering that being allowed to discuss emotions is very different to being expected to discuss emotions. People will talk when they're ready, when they feel safe, listened to and supported. I always say you should give people the benefit of the doubt – and often find that people are able to walk the line between honouring and remembering a lost love and embracing the chance of a new one, as long as everyone is prepared to respect different approaches. As we've seen already, living through grief isn't like watching sand slip through an hourglass: it's not going to finish neatly at a set time; it's more like sand on a beach, waves will wash across it, but you can keep walking over it.

It can also be a great help to share experiences with others who've been down this road. Debbie McGee told me that, although Paul Daniels had been the absolute love of her life, if she were to meet a new companion, she would now be open to this. 'I've already had my great love,' she said, 'and I don't ever need that again. I go on dates and have fun with friends, and yes, I believe that maybe there might be some-one else for me, but it will never take away from what I've already had. I could never replace Paul.' That hits the nail on the head for me – a new relationship doesn't lessen the one you had.

We're back to where we started – the words we use to talk about love. When people say they've already experienced the love of their life, it suggests that another partner after that would have to be some kind of second prize. But is that the reality? Not according to my friend Rachel. Harry was a great love – but that doesn't diminish her feelings for her new partner. 'He's not second prize,' she insisted after I put that to her. 'I love him with all my heart. I can't explain it other than to say it's different.'

Don't be afraid of the whispers of others too. Rachel said she'd heard it all: 'poor Harry's barely cold in his grave', and 'she hasn't given poor Harry a second thought'.

'None of that was true,' Rachel said, 'but it still hurt. The thing is, Harry knew me like nobody else did, and I knew him. He would be beaming with pride that I'm smiling again, that I didn't drown in my grief like I thought I would.'

That brings me to a truth we could have in almost every chapter of this book. Love is not finite, you don't run out of love, even if you run out of time together. That's partly why grief can be so intense and long-lasting – but it should also give us hope that we can love again.

I decided to do some online research into this and had to have a bit of a giggle when I came across a paper written by a clinician. There was a bit in there about one of her grief sessions, and a middle-aged guy had asked, 'if I were to bring a date home, how many pictures of my deceased wife would be too many?' The doctor had laughed and asked, 'well, if you went back to her home, how many pictures of her deceased husband would be too many?' The guy had laughed back and accepted that perhaps some of his shrine ought to come down. Of course, anyone would expect some photos and mementoes on the wall – but you'd hope that, by the time someone is dating again, the pictures prompt fond memories, not distress

There definitely is hope for anyone to find a new love after loss, and I think that if you want it, you should let it in. My advice: if you think you're ready, get out there and have a few dates. Don't have too many expectations and just go with the flow. Try to understand that others may try to put you off because they may feel it's too soon, or you're not ready. Just gently point out to them that you are ready to experience some happiness again, and assure them that you know what you're doing. It's a complicated time, and grief has changed you in some ways, so take your time to explore the new you with new people, and do try to enjoy the experience if it calls to you.

We all deserve love and happiness, after all. But it's true that comes in many forms. Those who choose to remain single after losing their partner are making an equally valid choice. If you feel your life is enriched enough and you have people around you who make you feel cherished and valued, or your work fulfils you, then that can be the right path for you. Just know that, if you are open to it, you could find another great love. And, of course, remember that great love may come in unexpected ways – platonic as well romantic love. New friendships, new family members or even a new pet. It is surprising how our hearts can grow, even when we were sure they were broken forever. Love is often where we least expect it to be.

To Love Again

I know when we were younger, and in the throes of love,
We lay entwined, made promises, beneath the stars above.
We swore that if one were to die and left behind the other,
We'd stay forever single, and could never love another.

But the years went by and our wild love grew into so much more,
With respect and understanding and contentment at the core.
We always knew there'd come a day when one of us would leave,
And the other one would be bereft, left all alone to grieve.

Our love was such that as we aged, we made a different oath,
We'd lived a life of happiness, of fulfilment and of growth.
We promised that whoever passed, the other who'd remain,
Would know that love is boundless, could withstand all the pain.

And so we'd know that as a loving soul, we'd still have much to give,
We gave each other permission to carry on and live.
We would still grieve, we'd mourn and cry and then
We'd open up our hearts and know we might love again.

Chapter 21

MOVING
FORWARD

I DELIBERATELY CALLED this chapter *Moving Forward* rather than *Moving On*, because carrying on with your life doesn't mean forgetting the one you've lost. After all, we often talk about the 'shadow' of death and I think you can either choose to stay still in that shadow, that tricky place where everything feels colder and darker than it used to, or accept that we all have a shadow, and yes, it's part of us, but it doesn't stop us stepping out into the sun.

What embracing your new normal means, though, is so individual. It's tightly related to the nature of your loss, how resilient you are at that time, your personality, other events you have to deal with and what support networks you have in place to assist you when the hard times hit. But at least by the time you're thinking about moving forward, you can accept, now, that your life is forever changed, and perhaps while you never stop wishing that everything could go back to how it used to be, you realise that can't happen, and you find the courage to look forward rather than back. I watched the whole of the Netflix series *After Life* recently. In it,

Ricky Gervais plays Tony, a character who loses his beloved wife of twenty-five years. There's a line in it where Tony says, 'we're not just here for us, we're here for others', and he says it at a time when he is finally able to accept that his wife has gone and he no longer feels suicidal about it. I think that line sums up all of our grief, really, when we are coming out the other side. It's a realisation that we can't remain in our own hurt bubble any longer. There are things that need doing, people who rely on us, and like it or not, we have a life and it must be lived.

It also takes time and strength to realise you're not just healing for yourself, you're healing for everyone around you. So while it's hard not be furious when people expect you to be putting the loss behind you and living life just as you did before, you can prepare yourself for how to tackle that thoughtless response. You might come across it in other forms too. You'll find the same mentality when people ask things like, 'are you still sad?' or 'haven't you moved past that yet?'. Sadly, some people only discover the real nature of grief when they go through it themselves.

So, do accept you're not moving past anything, nor are you leaving something behind you. Instead, you're finding the strength to pick up your sorrow and take it with you on your journey, and let it become part of what defines you – but not the whole.

Moving forward we learn to incorporate the loss into our present and recognise it will still be with us in our future but that we can handle it. It is accepting that getting over it isn't a goal, nor is it a healthy mindset. Our grief changes us, and moving forward means that we're letting ourselves and the world meet that new person.

I think of this point like the sun breaking out from behind the clouds. It can feel like a warm ray of light when you start to feel moments of positivity. You find yourself having flashes where you can think of who you've lost and be glad for having known them, rather than felled by the grief. You'll always be sad they won't be in your future, but you can start to contemplate the notion of the future again. And just like the sun through the clouds, those moments pass – but knowing they will come again can be enough to get you through.

This period is covered by those two extra stages of grief: reconstruction and working through, and acceptance and hope. That's why in the very first chapter I mentioned that these were very positive stages, and signal the coming light after the dark. A Cruse Bereavement counsellor told me: 'People say that time heals, but time doesn't heal, we do. We eventually learn how to live life differently, and it can be a wonderful life, filled with joy and love, it's just different, it's just a life without them by our side, but they'll always be in our hearts.'

Some people describe this moment as a bolt from the blue. They wake up one day and feel like they have the strength to face the day. Or perhaps they have a few hours before they realise they haven't thought about their loved one, and that is the start of them knowing that actually they can live a happy life again, just a different life. They start to be able to share memories – often funny ones – without feeling unbearably sad or going back into full-blown grief. Some describe that the deep sadness, the emptiness they have carried, is replaced by a sense of being back in the world – you've smashed the glass separating you from 'normal' life.

This is a time to invest in new connections. Be open to accepting new friendships. You may find that, despite initial reluctance, you actually enjoy completely new things. Music or books that never interested you before, a new genre of movies or TV. Take on some courses, embrace a lifelong learning attitude. Moving forward means that a whole new world is opening up to you, and you can be part of it. None of this means that you are forgetting the person you lost, or the person you were when they were here, it just means that you are finally ready to live again, but this time, as just you. The new you.

You might feel afraid at first, and this is completely normal, but hey, look what you've just been through. So what you're contemplating now will be a walk in the park compared to that. During this period you can test out talking about your loss now that it's not like looking up at a cliff-face, and perhaps you'll find that, rather than speaking about your grief, you'll be sharing memories and plans in equal measure. There will be the odd day of course when you might feel a pang of guilt because it's been days since you really thought about them, but in those times, rather than running away to hide, you'll realise that the loss will actually always be there, there is no expiry date, and it's okay to have days when your loved one isn't at the forefront of your mind. Grief is such an overwhelming state that your whole brain and body need time to heal, and after being on red alert for so long, it can be refreshing to let yourself take in the small things – enjoy a beautiful view, let yourself notice how the rain feels, celebrate a perfect cup of tea. Whatever it is, just be in the here and now after so long trying to keep afloat while having to fight off huge thoughts about your past and future. Sometimes, a deep breath is all you need to be in the moment.

The death of someone close tends to make us take a deep, introspective examination of our own lives, as we've explored. We have been touched by the fragility of it all, and although this can be a frightening experience, the experts at Co-op Funeralcare and Cruise Bereavement have told me that many people are surprised to learn that getting through grief can have a profoundly positive effect.

'Some people have told me that they decide to grab every opportunity life offers them,' Yolanda told me. 'They decide that life is far too short and far too precious to waste, and make lots of changes in their everyday routine.'

She went on to explain that this could be simple lifestyle changes such as eating better or taking more exercise. Some have made much bigger changes like giving up smoking, drinking or gambling, or anything they now perceive as a waste. And I personally know people who have gone even further than that and set out on a quest to do all the once-in-a-lifetime activities they'd always dreamed about but never dared to do: from running a marathon and bungee jumping for charity, to visiting far-off exotic lands. In fact, there's really nothing you can't do if you put your mind to it, and now is the time to start exploring all of that.

You should be proud of the strength you've shown. By making it through to this point, one day you'll be the person who knows what to say to someone in the first thunderstorm of loss. In the end, that's all we can do – pass on what we've learned and step into each day with hope, honesty and kindness.

To the future

I'm not getting over it but getting on,
Not walking past but walking with,
I'm faced the hardest truths on death,
But accepting I can live.

I'm not better but I'm stronger,
And balance darkness with the light,
Let good days bloom amid the bad,
And know I can fight this fight.

I can smile as well as cry,
Find joy as well as sorrow,
And not forget our yesterdays
But find hope for tomorrow.

Chapter 22

LOSING A PET

ARE YOU AN animal person? Dog-mad or a cat parent? It doesn't really matter what kind of animal it is, but if you've shared your life with a pet, it's likely you'll have built a bond that's unlike any other. A lot of people don't realise that grieving for a family pet can be just as painful and just as prolonged as grieving a relative. The hardest part of this is that others may expect you to get over an animal a lot quicker than you would a human, but this often isn't true. That pet was part of your life and shared every aspect of it with you. Just like a child, it was completely reliant on you for food, warmth, love and attention and was a huge part of your world. Many people spend more time with their pet than any other one person in their lives. The loss can be enormous and you can feel very alone in your grief, especially if you feel you can't share it.

I'm devoted to my pets – and I know just how much of your heart they steal, and the space they leave when you lose them. It's not just the love they show that bonds us to them, but their quirks and eccentricities – whether they're a grumpy goat or a faithful dog. They're often who we turn to in sadness, too. When a grieving friend of mine lost her husband she told me how hard she found it to get to sleep – the bed felt so cold and empty, until her cat sensed her pain and despite never having slept in the bed before, took to settling down beside her owner when she needed her the most.

Shirley, who I spoke about earlier, also spoke of her grief after losing their beloved dog, Charlie. 'He was 15,' she said, 'and had gone from being a cheeky little thing, always up to mischief, to like a little old man in a matter of weeks. We knew it was serious, and I think the day my husband Keith finally took him to the vets, I cuddled him that bit closer, and I cried my eyes out as they got into the car. I knew I'd never see our Charlie again. Oh, I cried for weeks, and we both swore we'd never get another pet again, we could never replace him.'

They did replace him, but it wasn't their doing. After Charlie had been gone almost a year, Shirley still missed him terribly, and the simplest thing would set her off crying again.

'I'd be looking for something and come across one of his raggedy old teddies,' she said, 'and that was it, I was in floods of tears again and pining for him. I think the grandkids must have been fed up of my moping because, despite me saying we'd never have another pet, our eldest turned up one day with another little puppy, exactly the same breed and colouring as Charlie. She'd put him a little flat cap and a bow tie on.

I fell in love with him immediately of course, and now our little Oscar is 6 and we wouldn't be without him.'

The pain you feel after losing a cherished pet can be truly overwhelming, and while others may not be able to comprehend just how much it hurts, you should never feel guilty or silly for grieving your animal friend. As with any other form of loss, we all grieve differently and it's exactly the same with a pet. A lot depends on the circumstances of their death, but however they left us, it will leave a gaping hole. In general, the more important your pet was to you, the more intensely you will grieve.

If your pet was a working animal, such as a service dog or therapy pet, you won't only be mourning the loss of your companion, but your support too. Perhaps your loss of independence or emotional support. If you live alone and your pet was your only companion, this can make the loss even harder to bear. Some people have said that they felt doubly traumatised because they had been unable to afford expensive treatments or operations to prolong their pet's life. Whatever your circumstances, no one can deny that, to a pet lover, the grief that follows after losing them can be as crushing as if they'd lost anybody else they loved. People say that experiencing such a loss is an inevitable part of owning a pet, but this knowledge doesn't make it any easier when the time comes.

I spoke to a vet friend of mine, Carla, and asked her what advice she has to help people grieving for their lost pet.

'Ritual seem to help,' she said. 'Regardless of whether others think it's inappropriate, a burial or little service for your pet, where the family can say goodbye out loud and share a fond memory or two, can be a huge help in the healing process, especially for children.'

Carla went on to say that some people get a lot of comfort by getting some kind of memorial for their pet. I was surprised to find out that there are vets and businesses that provide all kinds of beautiful things, such as glass engravings, a photograph etched onto a memory stone, cushions with photographs and rainbow bridge ornaments with a pet's name engraved on them. There are so many lovely ideas out there, and something might feel just right to you. I know one devastated pet owner who found some comfort in donating to a local dog's home. They weren't ready for a new pet themselves – but they could still help others even in their sorrow.

'It's important also to try to create a routine for any other pets in the household,' Carla pointed out, 'because they can also be grieving the loss of their buddy. I've known some owners tell me their left-behind pets seem depressed and won't eat. It's not surprising, really – they will be searching for a playmate who is no longer there. So, yes, even though you won't be feeling much like playing fetch with another pet, it is important that you force yourself to keep life as normal as possible for them. Take them for extra walks too if you can. It will not only be good for them, but it will be uplifting for you too.'

There are also online support groups for grieving pet owners, so if you've not got anyone in your immediate circle who understands what you're facing, it's well worth joining one of those forums so that you can speak with others who know just what you're going through. Or if you have friends who've also lost a pet, reach out to them because they, more than anyone else, will understand and be able to support you.

It is particularly hard for your child when a pet dies, as this is often their very first experience of personal loss and they can sometimes struggle to cope. If it was a natural passing, try to reassure them that it was nobody's fault and then explain to them what has happened as truthfully as you can. Some parents are often tempted to tell a story, suggest their pet has gone to a farm somewhere or even tell a lie to save hurt feelings, but none of this is really helpful. They need a way to say goodbye too. It's better to be honest and allow your child to go through the emotions they will be feeling. They may even be afraid that you, the parent, might also die and you need to tell them this won't happen. Get them to talk about their worries and address each one as it arises, but be as honest as possible. It might be some time before they are brave enough to get another pet, but again, reassure them it wouldn't be a replacement, but another friend to love and look after. If it's possible, include your child in a pet funeral or memorial. This helps them to open up and put words to how they feel.

Of course, it can go the other way too. Children can be incredibly resilient – even funny – in the hard times! I've known children compose poems in honour of a hamster, or even belt out 'Circle of Life' as their goldfish is buried. Their hope and good humour can be a huge strength.

If you feel you aren't sure whether to invite another pet into your home after suffering a loss, it's important not to focus on their lifespan and how you'd feel if it happened again. Instead focus on all the love you would share throughout their lifetime just as you did with your lost pet. If you're still unsure, then it would be wise to test yourself a little first. Offer to pet-sit for a friend or family member, or visit the local kennels or sanctuary and spend some time allowing yourself to be around them for a while. Most of all, ask yourself the question that matters most: could we give an animal the love and care it needs to thrive? If it's a yes, perhaps you're ready. I know we all say: never again! But as a huge pet lover myself, I know that some day we give in to our natures and we get to experience that love all over again.

For a Much-Loved Pet

Go run fast and free, my beloved and trusty friend,
Up and find that special place, where 'go fetch' will never end.
I'll see you in another life, and you'll be watching out for me,
You'll cover me in kisses and I'll shout out with glee.

You were so much more than just a pet, you were my everything,
Now run across the rainbow bridge to where it's always spring.
Go play with all the other dogs, and when the time is right,
Cross it back the other way, for when we reunite.

Chapter 23

HOSPICE CARE

I THOUGHT LONG and hard about including this next chapter as it doesn't directly relate to grief, more what comes before. However, throughout this book we have covered many of the ways in which our loved ones die, and touched on being with them at the end. For people who choose hospice care for their final weeks or days, they are choosing – or their family are choosing for them – a dignified ending in a care setting where loved ones can come and go as regularly as they like and to be there during the last moments if that's what they all want. Whilst most people don't want to die alone, and would like to be surrounded by loved ones at the end, others prefer to be alone at this point, perhaps to spare their loved ones having to witness it.

We don't all have the choice about where we or our loved ones spend our last days, even if we know they're coming. Sometimes it's possible to be at home; others might be unable to leave hospital. We think of hospitals as places of diagnosis and treatment – but modern hospitals often have holistic functions too, and of course there will also be a prayer space and often a chaplain or other faith leader too. But lots of people who do have the choice opt for a hospice.

People assume hospices are sad places, but if you've visited a friend or relative in a modern hospice, I'm sure like me you'll have been amazed by what loving, caring places they are, staffed by some of the most caring people I've had the privilege to meet. If a friend or family member is receiving hospice care, please don't feel apprehensive about visiting – they're welcoming and inspirational places.

Some hospice providers are funded by the NHS and others by donations, but in the UK, hospice care is free. Although you can phone them directly to ask about a place, you will then need a GP or nurse referral. The service offered by a hospice is not only for end of life care, but for medical and emotional support at any stage through a terminal illness, and the surroundings are far less clinical than most other medical environments.

Hospices offer many different types of care, depending on your situation. It might be:

- Visiting a hospice for day care
- Staying at a hospice for a few days or weeks and then returning home after care
- Receiving hospice care at home, where the nurses visit you
- Staying in a hospice for the last days or weeks of your life
- Going to a hospice for a respite period so that your carers at home get a break

Whichever way you access a hospice, you will have a host of medical professionals on hand, such as doctors, specialist nurses, occupational therapists and physiotherapists, as well as healthcare assistants who can help with personal care, and a variety of complimentary therapists who can help ease symptoms using techniques such as massage, reflexology and aromatherapy – all of which are proven to assist with pain relief, alongside conventional medicine. They really do focus on quality of life and are completely patient-centred.

Another important aspect of hospice care is emotional support. Counsellors are on hand to offer you the space to talk through your feelings and any fears you might have. Priests, chaplains and spiritual advisors are also available for you to discuss your faith with, including any fears or beliefs you have about dying. In some hospice settings there may also be art therapists available so that you can express your feelings through a creative outlet.

They are also practical places – there's usually access to a social worker who can assist you with any worries about benefits you or your family might be entitled to. There are no questions off-limits. And I think a lot of that is down to the amazing teams that work in them.

My friend Bridget is a Marie Curie nurse, part of an incredible organisation that really helps to demystify end of life care. They offer support to countless patients at home and they also run hospices. It's in one of their hospices that

Bridget works, providing palliative care to patients. I think that phrase alone sometimes sounds more complicated than it is – palliative care really just means treating a condition to make the patient more comfortable even if the treatment can't cure things.

I know that many of us are in awe of the nurses who help us or our families when we get the worse of news, and find it hard to imagine working with ill patients and having to care for people who you know won't get better. I think most medics will acknowledge that yes, it is incredibly hard – but the reward of helping people through those toughest of times makes it all worthwhile.

A lot of people ask Bridget how she has the strength to do what she does. She has spent many years caring for those nearing the end, and she always tells people who ask that she really loves her job.

'I see it as a privilege,' she said, 'that my patients share so much and allow me to know them so closely and often we become really good friends before they pass.'

'Isn't that hard?' I asked. 'Doesn't it make you sad that you have to go through bereavement so often?' I couldn't imagine being able to cope with such loss regularly.

'Not in the way you might think,' Bridget said. 'My sadness is reserved for those left behind, really. It's they who need the support afterwards. Not so much for my patients because we're so focussed on giving them the very best care, and often by the end, they've accepted it and are relieved to be able to leave this life with as much say in things as possible.' Bridget sighed and smiled at me. 'You know, it might sound strange but it can be a special experience, being there in those final moments.'

'Special?' I asked. 'How?'

'Well, people often share some incredible insights. I think it shows you how generous people can be even at the end – thinking about what they can pass on. I've been given all sorts of advice and insight.'

'What are some of the most memorable?' I asked.

'Well, lots of them make me smile,' Bridget told me. 'From people who tell me the secret is to never stop having fun, to those who say that they've made their peace and want to go out of this world with a smile on their face. I mean, how strong some people can be.'

'Do any of your patients ever tell you about any regrets they have?' I asked. This was something I'd always wondered about.

Bridget nodded. 'Do you know, there's a few things that come up time and again. The top one seems to be they regret not living a life true to themselves but feel instead they spent too long trying to fit in with what was expected of them. Next seems to be not making amends with people they've fallen out with, and not expressing their love freely and more often, and the third most common regret I've heard is not doing the things they always said they would do some day. I do find at the end what matters to people is the people and passions they care about, not possessions. I'm lucky to hear about people's great loves – whether it's their family, their love of music or travel, or one patient who wanted one last glass of wine! And then of course there are the funny ones that I think I've learned to take to heart – no one ever told me they wished they'd spent more time dieting or dusting!'

'Wow!' I said. 'Well that's a lesson for us all, I think. Is there anything else you can tell us? Something we probably wouldn't know?'

'It might surprise you, but there are three things about death that most people – including myself at the start of my career – aren't aware of,' Bridget said. 'The first is that during the unconscious stage, hours or sometimes even a day or two before death, the common belief is that they can't hear. We, and most professionals these days, believe this to be untrue. Research has proven that hearing is often the last sense to go, and although normal communication can't take place, the patient may still be able to hear and know who is in the room with them. We always encourage family and visitors to speak gently as if their loved one can hear what is being said, and to definitely not speak about them as if they can't. At the end of life it's really just about being present, and providing an atmosphere that's comforting to the one dying.'

'What a comforting thought. And the second thing?' I asked.

'Hydration,' Bridget said. 'This might be hard to hear, but as a nurse, it's a topic we're well trained in. There's a significant amount of family members who try to insist that we feed or give drinks to those who no longer want it. The thing is, the body is actually built to die and, believe it or not, dehydration helps us to have a more peaceful death. If we try to hydrate a dying body, it will become overloaded with fluid and eventually go into respiratory distress because it can't handle the fluids. So, it's definitely far kinder to withdraw liquids at the very end to assist the process and make it easier for the patient.'

I'd never heard that before; I think many of us still think of those last days and hours as playing out like they would in a TV hospital show, but in real life and death, the nurses are there to make things undramatic, gentle, thoughtful, peaceful. But there can still be surprises.

'Yes, the third thing that might shock you is the resilience of a dying person right at the end. Sometimes family members witness this sudden burst of energy and believe that their loved one is starting to get a bit better. This is part of what's known as deathbed phenomena, and it's one of the most mysterious parts of the process because it's so hard to study. But from what we observe, this last phase can sometimes involve all kinds of unusual states. Some of these, scientists have been able to investigate, while others are still unexplained.

'It's definitely quite mysterious,' Bridget said. 'We're so used to taking statistics and measurements, but in the final stages of dying, in more cases than I can remember, there are behaviours and responses we can't yet understand. Visions are a huge part of these – often the patients appear to see and hear their own lost loved ones. They talk to them, smile and become quite animated. It's amazing to witness.'

'And what do you think?' I asked. 'As a nurse, do you believe they are actually seeing ghosts?'

'I'm not sure what it is,' Bridget admitted, 'but the brain is a wonderful thing, isn't it? Even at the end of life it is trying to teach us and protect us, I guess. I don't feel it matters if it's real or not. I've seen my patients almost euphoric when they feel someone from their past has come along to guide them to another place.'

'I can see how all this might be strangely comforting to you too,' I said, understanding now why Bridget had described her job as being extraordinary.

'It is,' she said. 'I don't fear death at all doing the job I do, and being able to help people do things their way is an honour. Some patients fight, and I mean really fight, to stay alive until their loved ones get there to share their final moments, and then they allow themselves to pass. Others seem to actively fight to stay alive until all the family have left, and then die, peacefully, alone. It's a final choice some people get to make.'

This led me to think about all those times we hear of a family's devastation that they didn't get to their loved one in time before they died. But perhaps their loved one had always planned this. 'Do you think that this is intentional in some cases?' I asked Bridget.

'I know it is,' Bridget said. 'I've been told so many times by my patients that, despite the family's wishes, they intend to do that final bit alone.'

I learned such a lot by speaking to hospice carers, especially to Bridget, about how death can be made to feel like a natural part of life, if we're not afraid to be honest with people, if we're able to honour people's wishes, and if the medical staff are able to share some of their hard-won wisdom and experiences with the families of the dying so they feel less overwhelmed by the enormity of what they're going through.

Like most people, I thought the word 'hospice' was a scary one and implied imminent death. I don't think this now. I think it's wonderful that many of us have access to such a caring and peaceful facility when we need it the most.

To share this time with you

I want to sit with you awhile, just sit and watch you breathe,
I'm in awe of how at peace you are, as you prepare to leave.
You told me that you've said goodbye to all you leave behind,
You've made amends, told some truths, and now
have peace of mind.

You grip my hand from time to time and I wonder if you fear,
What comes next on your great journey as you leave us here.
But I see you smile as you speak words to people I can't see,
You reach to touch those unseen friends as you let go of me.

Your breathing slows and you relax, you almost look serene,
Your pain has gone, I see that now, I do not intervene.
I will remain with you awhile, you wanted me to stay,
It was such a privilege to sit with you, to see you on your way.

Chapter 24

WHAT NEXT?

WHEN WE TALK about death, we often avoid the D-word itself. It's partly out of fear, partly out of sensitivity, and perhaps also slightly out of superstition. But it's also because, as much as we know it's coming, we all know that living in the present is the only way life can truly be experienced. Of course, we're shaped by our memories and should plan for our futures, but we're only ever really alive in the current moment. So, in the middle of our busy complicated lives, when we do think about what comes next, we'll often turn to the wisdom of others – whether we find that in faith, art or science.

So many of the famous quotes about the end of life are naturally about the biggest mystery – what comes next? Whether it's Shakespeare's 'the undiscovered country' of Hamlet or Eric Clapton's 'Tears in Heaven', our artists and poets often ask the question about what happens beyond life's horizon. Mother Teresa famously said, 'death is nothing else but going home to God, the bond of love will be unbroken for all eternity.' Perhaps the most poignant quote

I've heard came from blind American author, Helen Keller. She said, 'death is no more than passing from one room into another. But, there's a difference for me, you know, because in that room I shall be able to see'.

For some people faith gives a framework – whether that's the belief that your loved one is in heaven, or that their essence will return to earth in another life. The origins of the notion of reincarnation are obscure but they go back millennia. Discussion of the subject appears in the philosophical traditions of Ancient India. The Greek Pre-Socratics discussed reincarnation, and the Celtic druids are also reported to have taught a doctrine of reincarnation. Wherever the idea originally came from, it essentially means the rebirth of the soul in another body, and the notion brings comfort to those who believe in it.

For other people it might even be a sense of a spirit life that provides comfort and structure at passing – it's a set of beliefs that occurs all over the world, whether it's returning spirits seven nights after death in Chinese culture or the Mexican Day of the Dead, there are so many ways that people feel that death is not the end.

A common view is that after death the soul ascends to heaven to be reunited with a God, our maker. Whether you're religious or not, I think it's powerful to understand that people have been struggling to make sense of death since our earliest records. Perhaps we shouldn't be surprised since it's not just humans that mourn. I'm sure we've all seen the incredible, heartrending footage of animals that are grieving – from elephant graveyards to chimpanzees mourning the loss of a family member. It seems that so many creatures, not just us people, find it hard to comprehend that life is often as fragile as it is precious.

Others are certain about the lack of existence after death and find that this makes life all the more beautiful for its fleeting nature. If you've ever been to a Humanist funeral you'll know that even without traditional structures of hymns or resting in heaven, there can be incredible comfort in the words spoken, in the shared acknowledgement that even if death is seen as the end, it doesn't mean the service can't be full of joy and peace. For those that believe the meaning of life lies not in religious belief but in doing good on earth for your fellow man, then there is great support in coming together to mark someone's passing.

For other people, they may have no formal religion, but grief can lead them to a different, personal kind of spirituality. For some of these people, mediums can give a sense of continuation. We all know someone who has sought answers by visiting, calling or contacting a medium or spiritualist. The hope that their loved one will come through with a message for them is a strong urge and, if they hear something that meets their needs, it can bring an enormous amount of comfort to believe that there is more to life and death than we can understand.

Whether you think of Derek Acorah or Doris Stokes when you hear about mediums, you've probably heard or seen some of the people who have become famous attempting to reach through the veil they feel separates life and death. Stokes, for instance, was a prolific writer and a renowned medium who found global audiences. Her professed ability to communicate with the dead, her public appearances and memoirs made her a household name and I know she brought comfort to many, many people, despite others remaining sceptical. But it's a phenomenon that goes back centuries – from ancient shamans to Victorian seances. If you are one of the people drawn to try to communicate via a medium, and it helps you, then take the support you need, but not at the expense of living your life. Take comfort in the fact that, as well as relying on psychics and spiritualists, it's also possible to let your loved one live on in your memories and those of others and commemorate their life in some way.

My own thoughts are that if we can accept that none of us can really know for sure what happens in and after those last moments of life, then it's okay to accept that people will have their own beliefs, and if they can bring comfort then surely that's a wonderful thing, even if their beliefs don't match our own. The truth is that whether we sign up to the idea of an afterlife or not, we really do live on within the people we influence whilst we are living.

I also feel that science and religion shouldn't be set as opposites – it doesn't have to be an either/or. In fact, I love that the laws of physics tell us that energy cannot be either created or destroyed – only transformed.

Another kind of life beyond death is one that I know many people find hard to discuss, but can be one of the most lifechanging choices we ever make. The generosity that many people show as their last act by carrying a donor card is one of the most selfless of gifts. It can be a hard topic to broach, so if it's important to you, do sign up. Then, after doing that, make sure you tell your loved ones what you've done so that they don't have to make any difficult choices on your behalf.

The gift of hope is another way you can change lives even after you've passed on. My sister, Bernie, was an ambassador for Breakthrough Breast Cancer before she died, and they set up a fundraising tribute fund in honour of her. It's lovely to think that, even though she's gone, her impact lives on and people can continue her fight against this disease for many years to come.

I wonder

I wonder where my soul goes, when I leave this life I know,
Will it slip gently from my being, will I feel the letting go?
Will my soul live on in some other place or plane,
Will I know what's happening, will I be free from pain?
Will I watch over those I've left, as is so often thought,
It sounds a comfort, yet I'd be sad to see them all distraught.
Or might I be reborn, return a different person,
Just flashbacks of an old me, though I rather like this version.
I can wonder where my soul goes, and what becomes of me,
But it's rhetorical, for more than that we're never meant to see.
It's one last great adventure, towards the vast unknown,
And maybe I'll know it when I see it, that my soul is going home.

Chapter 25

WHAT DO I SAY?

ALL THROUGH THIS book we've touched on times when words don't come easily. If you've just been bereaved, then even finding the words to say that out loud is incredibly tough. It's a difficult truth that, while you're struggling to come to terms with what's happened, one of the first things you need to do is tell other people.

I was talking to a friend who told me about losing her dad unexpectedly. You often feel powerless in the face of a sudden death, and for her, as hard as it was, one of the only practical things she could do to help her family was to make those difficult calls to friends and wider family to share the devastating news. There's a reason why the old clichés exist about getting bad news: 'you might want to sit down for this' holds true because people can literally feel faint when they have to process the news. But, as hard as it can be, sharing this sad news in person or over the phone – speaking those words – might help you start to process the fact that your loss is real, not just some bad dream. These days, people often share the news to broader circles by text or social media – the modern equivalent of putting a death notice in the paper. It can seem impersonal but I do think it's worth doing as people do want to know, do want to offer support, and it's good to know that your loved one touched so many other lives.

Once you've managed to share the news, however, you might find varying kinds of responses after the immediate condolences: those people in your life who can't even make eye contact, let alone mention what you're going through, and those who seem to have no filter and will ask you for details, or ask you why you're not 'over it'. It's hard not to blow your top or dissolve into tears at some of these conversations – and people will understand you're on an emotional seesaw – but it can help to prepare a stock answer to questions if you know you find it too hard to think on the spot. But please, don't tell people you're 'fine'! You're probably lots of things – angry, heartbroken, relieved, guilty, lonely, confused, coping or struggling. So don't feel you have to hide behind 'fine' if you're not there yet.

But what about if you're supporting someone who's going through grief – what could or should you say?

For me, the main thing I've learned is to read each situation for itself. How can you acknowledge someone's loss in a way that feels appropriate, supportive but not traumatising? As I touched on earlier, the key thing is not to ignore the topic. Don't be afraid of using 'standard' phrases: 'I'm sorry for your loss' or 'may their memory be a blessing' are common reactions for some people, and it shows you're not afraid to raise the issue. But then after you've said something, the most important part can be to listen to the reply. They might acknowledge it and move on – not everyone wants to discuss their grief at all times. Or they might be really glad you've mentioned it and want to open up or share memories or stories. Take their lead and show them you're not afraid of their emotions.

Your first contact with your grieving friend or relative might not be in person or even on the phone, of course. I know a lot of people stay quiet because they feel awkward and think it safe to assume that their grieving friend needs some time and space. I think it never hurts to reach out, though we should try not to second-guess how someone is feeling. Yes, some people will want some peace and solitude to come to terms with their loss, but others might rather be busy and welcome a visit, call or even just a distraction from the scale of their feelings. Don't stop inviting people to things – you never know what they might find therapeutic: maybe a good singalong at a gig, a chance to punch it out at a boxing class or even just a cuppa in the local café could be the reason someone needs to get up and face the world.

If you're not sure how to contact someone you know is grieving, then why not send a card or letter? Lots of us have got out of the habit of sending actual notes now everyone's on email, but there's something really thoughtful about a personally chosen card or handwritten letter. It's a physical sign that someone's thinking about you. Of course, a card might seem insignificant in the face of grief, but often people say that, when they're starting to feel a bit better, they go back to look at the cards and letters people sent and it feels like someone's giving them a hug from far away.

Don't stay silent out of fear of saying the wrong thing! Even when people are in the deepest parts of grief they can usually tell when someone means well. Although there are a couple of phrases I'd recommend either avoiding or at least using with caution. I wrote earlier about how being 'in a better place' didn't sit well with me, and I asked a few friends what other common responses they found difficult. One friend told me that any reaction that started with 'at least . . .' got her goat. 'At least they didn't suffer' or 'at least you've got a big family'. It can feel like you're minimising their grief. Another friend said what she hates is something she calls 'grief bingo'! Of course, it can be really supportive when people share their own experiences with you – if someone else has lost a parent while you're grieving your own, you might feel they understand something of what you're going through. But if it seems like competitive griev-ing – someone shouting out their own losses (especially if they're not close ones) – it can feel like they don't really want to hear about anyone else's experiences. My friend said she'd told a colleague about how she was feeling after losing her mum, only for her coworker to compare it to how they felt when the Queen Mother died.

One thing I've learned from personal experience is that being specific can be really helpful. When someone's grieving, everything often feels terrifyingly big – from feelings to practicalities, there can be so much to cope with that everything grinds to a halt. So if you ask someone how they are, they might not even know where to begin. But if you ask how they are today, that's an easier question to manage – it recognises there might be good days and bad days; it doesn't demand anything about the past and the future, just a window on their world right now.

This also made me think about the advice we often give to friends supporting new mothers. They're at the opposite end of the spectrum of life and death, but some of the best advice on how to help holds true! So, don't ask your grieving friend if there's anything you can do to help – that's just giving them an extra job or two trying to think a) what anyone can possibly do to make them feel better and b) can anyone actually provide the help they need.

Instead, why not try offering specific support? Ask if they'd like a visit, ask if they need anything while you're at the shops, ask if you can pop round or walk their dog. And most of all, don't be offended if they say no! Of course, when it comes to supporting friends or family, it's not something we ask once and then tick that box. Being ready to show your friends that they can talk about their grief in their own time is really important. Everyone processes emotion in their own way and may want a shoulder to cry on at surprising times, soon after or many months or even years later. Telling people you'll be there when they're ready not only shows that you're sticking around, but that it's okay for them to get there on their own schedule.

I often tell people that grief isn't catching. Yes, hearing someone newly bereaved share their experiences can make us think about our own times of mourning, but don't treat folk like they've got a disease! I wrote earlier about how people are likely to grieve in ways that are true to their character – whether they're outgoing or shy – and that can reflect how comfortable they find it to share their feelings after a loss. If you've got a friend or family member who needs to talk but finds it tricky, there are a few tactics I've found useful in the past.

My first trick is finding a no-pressure situation, and this often means one where you might not even be making eye contact. How often have you found that big conversations are easiest when you're in the car? Everyone's looking ahead at the road rather than staring at one another! You can get the same effect by taking a walk with someone – or even just being in the same room but giving them the time and space to open up. Another great way to let people feel you're there to listen – but not to put them under the microscope – is to chat while you're both doing something else. You might have heard of 'knit and natter' sessions for keen crafters; or how about sharing a simple activity that means you've got something else to focus on rather than anyone feeling pressure to ask or answer big questions? – doing a jigsaw together, perhaps, or I even heard from one friend that they found it easier to talk while gardening.

We've already looked at the soothing and healing power of art, and there are other great alternatives to conversation if that's too tough, such as watching a film together or joining a book club. I know of one friend who was worried her teenage son wasn't handling his grief over losing his grand-dad, until she realised, when he was on his computer, he was actually getting support from his gaming friends.

I find that whether you're the one grieving or the friend supporting, people do want to help. There's no antidote to grief – you'll often hear that there's no way to avoid it, it's something to be got through rather than hidden from – but sharing some of the burden is one way of making that journey less lonely.

I want you to know this

I'm devastated for you, so sorry for your loss,
I want to hug and comfort you, and be there, just because.
I know I'll never understand the hurt you're feeling now,
But I really want to be there, to help you through somehow.

We can simply sit in silence, or I'll hug you when you cry,
We could talk until the sun comes up, there's nothing I won't try.
You can share your anger, your memories or tears,
Tell me what you're thinking, your questions or your fears.

For now, I'll just walk with you, raise you up each time you fall,
For as long as you might need me, I'll be there through it all.
And if you want to be alone, I'll understand that too,
As long as you know come what may, I'm always here for you.

Chapter 26

WHERE CAN I TURN FOR HELP?

THROUGHOUT THIS BOOK I've mentioned quite a few organisations that can support us at different points on our journey: when we are learning about a diagnosis, when we are about to lose someone we love, in the intense first few days after a bereavement, when we need to plan a funeral or when a beloved pet passes away. And, of course, lots of these groups and charities are not just for that first acute phase, but for the weeks, months and years after when we might be tackling grief we'd packed away and not faced.

That first call or email can be a huge step and, if you're not ready to contact another person for support at the moment, do remember that help comes in all shapes and sizes. As well as my own series, there are some other brilliant podcasts out there where people share their stories, their advice and their coping strategies. And if you've found this book helpful, there are some other powerful reads that might help you along your journey. If you pop into your local library or bookshop, you'll find everything from practical self-help workbooks to memoirs by people who've come through profound loss.

There are some incredible forums on the internet too – but I would urge some caution here as we all know the internet is not always a kind place. If you've already got trusted communities, then do reach out – but if you're joining new social media sites or groups, do choose carefully. That's why I would recommend contacting some of the charities and organisations below as they can offer real, personal advice and support in some cases – or just a listening ear in others.

When you are ready, please do reach out, because honestly, they really do know what you're going through, and they really do want to help. We can only get so much input from family and friends, and in spite of their best efforts to understand, they might be too close to the situation, or grieving themselves, and that's when an expert can change everything for you and give you that extra support you might need.

Here I will list the ones I've already spoken about as well as some others that I think might be helpful. Please be aware that some of these details may change, so if you can't reach these teams via the details below, do remember that you can also find details of helpful organisations from most hospitals, coroners, Citizen's Advice, as well as libraries and GPs.

Samaritans

https://www.samaritans.org

Phone day or night: 116 123. Their website also has an instant chat facility.

Mission Statement: If you need someone to talk to, we listen. We won't judge or tell you what to do.

Co-op Funeralcare

https://www.coop.co.uk/funeralcare

Phone: 0808 303 2076. Available 24 hours a day, 7 days a week.

Co-op offers bereavement support, help with arranging a funeral and coping with all stages of grief.

Cruse Bereavement Support

https://www.cruse.org.uk/about/contact-us/

Phone: 0808 808 1677

Mission Statement: A world where everyone grieving is supported, respected and understood.

Child Bereavement UK

https://www.childbereavementuk.org/

Phone: 0800 02 888 40

Mission Statement: We help children, young people, parents, and families to rebuild their lives when a child grieves or when a child dies.

Marie Curie

https://www.mariecurie.org.uk/

Phone: 0800 090 2309

Mission statement: Whatever the illness, we're with you to the end. Everyone deserves the right support at the end of life. We're here for anyone with an illness they're likely to die from, and their family and friends.

Blue Cross – Pet Bereavement

https://www.bluecross.org.uk/pet-bereavement-and-pet-loss

Phone: 0800 096 6606. Their website also offers an online chat service up to 8.30pm

Mission Statement: Pet loss support. Here to take your hand when they let go.

Spiritualists

https://sagb.org.uk/mediums.htm

For those who believe in the continuation of the personality after physical death, and to relieve suffering through Spiritual Healing

Humanists UK

https://humanists.uk

For those who believe that, in the absence of an afterlife or God, human beings can act to give their own lives meaning by seeking happiness in this life and helping others to do the same.

NHS: Dealing with grief after bereavement
https://www.nhs.uk/mental-health/feelings-symptoms
-behaviours/feelings-and-symptoms/grief-bereavement-loss/

Hospice UK
https://www.hospiceuk.org
National charity for hospice and end of life care. This website has a postcode entry facility which directs you to the hospice closest to you. It also gives you all the information you might need.

MIND
https://www.mind.org.uk/information-support/types-of
-mental-health-problems/suicidal-feelings/useful-contacts/
This link will take you to a list of helpful phone numbers for anyone suffering from mental health issues or suicidal thoughts.

PAPYRUS UK – Prevention of Young Suicide
https://www.papyrus-uk.org
Call: 0800 068 4141 (HOPELINE247) for confidential support and practical advice. Lines are open 24 hours every day of the year. Text: 88247
Email: pat@papyrus-uk.org
Mission statement: Prevention of young suicide and supporting those affected by it

The Good Grief Trust

https://www.thegoodgrieftrust.org

Mission statement: A charity run by the bereaved for the bereaved

As well as the national organisations, The Good Grief Trust can connect you to local groups in your own area for face-to-face conversations and support.

AFTERWORD

I HOPE YOU have found this book helpful in some small way. I wrote it because I've been through so much of it myself and I know how difficult it can be. I know I'll need to take my own advice again in the future too – to help myself, friends and family. Most of us will take this grief journey more than once, and each time it will feel different.

I don't want you to ever feel alone, because I know that, even when you are surrounded by people, you can still feel desperately lonely when you have suffered a great loss.

Hopefully by reading through some of my experiences and those of my friends, you'll see that, while we are all going through unique circumstances and tackling it in our own way, there is something greater we have in common. To grieve is to have loved, and I really do feel love is part of what makes us human. Someone can have lived a totally different life in a different part of the world, they can have lost someone we never met, but we can know in our bones that they grieve as deeply as we have.

None of us will mourn at the same time in the same way, but we all feel grief just as powerfully as the next person, and as strange as it may sound, it is a superpower. The ability to feel deeply is a way of living life to the full – right up to the end, whenever and however it comes. Grief might be an iceberg – there's so much more beneath the surface that no one ever normally sees. But icebergs float and you too will surface from the sorrow, in your own style, in your own time. Your way is okay.

Love, Coleen x

ACKNOWLEDGMENTS

To Genevieve and all the gang at HarperNorth and HarperCollins. Thank you for trusting me with this book and for all your help and support.

To Julie Shaw . . . wow we got there in the end. Thank you for your guidance and for helping me to make sense of it all.

To everyone at Bold Management for your belief in me and always having my back. I'm so glad we met!

To all who've shared their stories for this book: experts, celebrity friends and colleagues, thank you for trusting me with your very personal journeys through grief . . . you're all amazing!

To my family, we've been through so much together over the years, but we always come out stronger! I love you so much.

To my children, Shane, Jake and Ciara. You are my world and my life. No words can possibly convey the love I have for you...it's beyond words!

To Michael, thank you for being a part of my crazy life. You are my calm and my peace. I love you.

Grief is always hard and sometimes it can feel unbearable. I hope this book helps you, even slightly, to move forward and realise that you never have to feel alone again with a hand to hold.

Harper
North

BOOK CREDITS

would like to thank the following staff and contributors
for their involvement in making this book a reality:

Alexandra Allden	Taslima Khatun
Fionnuala Barrett	Sammy Luton
Samuel Birkett	Rachel McCarron
Peter Borcsok	Molly McNevin
Ciara Briggs	Ben McConnell
Sarah Burke	Petra Moll
Alan Cracknell	Alice Murphy-Pyle
Jonathan de Peyer	Adam Murray
Anna Derkacz	Genevieve Pegg
Tom Dunstan	Amanda Percival
Kate Elton	Natasha Photiou
Sarah Emsley	Agnes Rigou
Simon Gerratt	Florence Shepherd
Monica Green	Eleanor Slater
Natassa Hadjinicolaou	Angela Snowden
CJ Harter	Emma Sullivan
Megan Jones	Katrina Troy
Jean-Marie Kelly	Daisy Watt

For more unmissable reads,
sign up to the HarperNorth newsletter at
www.harpernorth.co.uk

or find us on Twitter at
@HarperNorthUK

**Harper
North**